HOW TO GROW YOUR OWN MONEY

THE INEVITABLE (BUT IMPORTANT) DISCLAIMER

The contents of this book are for general use only and are not intended to address your specific personal circumstances. In particular, the information provided does not constitute any form of advice or recommendation by the publisher or the author and is not intended to be relied on when making or refraining from making any investment decisions. The value of investments can go down as well as up and favorable results are never assured, regardless of the techniques used, nor are any guarantees given. You should exercise caution when making any investment decision and any such decisions made by you are at your sole risk and responsibility.

HOW TO GROW YOUR OWN MONEY

The no-nonsense guide
for the independent investor

DAVID MECKIN

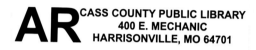

nb

NICHOLAS BREALEY
PUBLISHING

London • Boston

First published by
Nicholas Brealey Publishing in 2014

3–5 Spafield Street
Clerkenwell, London
EC1R 4QB, UK
Tel: +44 (0)20 7239 0360
Fax: +44 (0)20 7239 0370

20 Park Plaza
Boston
MA 02116, USA
Tel: (888) BREALEY
Fax: (617) 523 3708

www.nicholasbrealey.com
www.insight-investing.com

ISBN: 978-1-85788-614-6
eISBN: 978-1-85788-963-5

British Library Cataloguing in Publication Data
A catalogue record for this book is available from the
British Library.

Printed in Finland by Bookwell.

CONTENTS

Preface

A MANIFESTO FOR THE
INDEPENDENT INVESTOR

I t was supposed to be another of those annual reviews with my financial adviser where he tells me my investments are doing fine, I sign a few forms, and then get back to work, but this day was to prove different. About ten years previously I had invested $100,000 in a managed fund and now wanted to access the cash to help finance a new business venture. You can imagine my surprise when I was told that $90,000 would be in my bank account within the next few weeks. This led to a conversation, somewhat incredulous on my part, that went along the following lines.

"If I have got this right, in the space of ten years a professional fund manager has managed to turn $100,000 of my money into $90,000."

"Regrettably, this fund has not done particularly well."

"You're telling me! I'm assuming I haven't had to pay any fees for this debacle?"

"Fees are always applicable, I'm afraid; managing funds is a costly business."

"What fees are we talking about here?"

"Well, we receive a fee for providing you with advice and for introducing your business; then there's the fund manager, who charges a fee for managing your money; then there are a wide variety of administrative costs such as dealing charges (those are the costs of buying and selling shares within the fund); also let's not forget..."

"Just wait a moment. Over the past ten years you have received a fee, the fund manager has received a fee, and various other parties have been imposing charges as well, so the only person worse off on the deal is me!"

Keen to ascertain just how much I had been charged over the previous few years (and angry with myself for not having fathomed this out earlier), a little research on my part indicated that fees and expenses totaled somewhere in the region of $30,000. In other words, over the preceding ten years I had paid financial advisers, fund managers, and various other parties $30,000 to turn $100,000 of my money into $90,000. That is the difference between managing money and *growing* money.

The financial services sector offers to manage your money for you, and will charge you handsomely to do it, but that is not what investors want – all investors are interested in is seeing their money grow. Ironically, that is the one service the financial services sector will not promise to deliver; if it did, I would have been due a substantial refund. Fund managers just cannot lose. They are paid a basic salary, plus they are incentivized with a bonus if they can improve short-term profits, which encourages risk-taking. If a fund manager is looking after your money and loses it all, they still get paid. If they take risks with your money, providing short-term wins (possibly at the expense of long-term gains), they earn even more. That is when it dawned on me:

"Nobody cares more about your money than you do!"

These few words were about to change the way I approached investing for ever – that statement became my rallying cry and my mantra.

I decided it was time to take control – it was time to become an independent investor. Over the next few weeks I converted my various funds to cash and started out on a journey that has turned out to be one of the most stimulating, and ultimately profitable, of my life; and I don't mean purely in terms of money. When I talk about control, I don't only mean taking control of your finances, I mean taking control of your life. The whole point of investing is to help you attain the lifestyle you aspire to. Whether it's driving that dream car, living in that idyllic country cottage, or being able to travel and experience the joys of the world, investing can turn fantasy into reality.

And yet, despite the potential rewards, many investors feel powerless, particularly when they have a large sum to invest. They feel that they don't have the time, or the expertise, to invest independently, and that they have no alternative but to use the services of fund managers. The problem is, once they hand over their money, they are at the mercy of these individuals (and their fees). Maybe their fund will grow, maybe it won't – they themselves have very little control.

In this book we are going to discover how you can take back control – how you can become an independent investor and grow your own money.

This seems like an appropriate juncture to reveal a little about my background. I spent the first few years of my working life climbing the corporate ladder, ultimately achieving the position of finance director of a multinational group, but it had always been my goal to set up my own business. One thing I noticed in every company I worked for was the gulf that seemed to exist between the finance people and the managers who were running the business. As a result, the managers endeavored to steer well clear of financial issues wherever possible.

It struck me that there was an opportunity to improve the returns to shareholders by making managers aware of the financial implications of their decisions, so I set up my own consultancy to do just that. I also wrote my first book, *Naked Finance*, which demystifies the world of business finance. By stripping the topic down to its bare essentials, I wanted to show managers with no previous knowledge of finance, whether management trainees or main board directors, how they could make sound financial decisions. This book has a similar objective: to demystify the world of investing so that you can make sound investment decisions.

Soon my company expanded into the world of personal finance. I began running personal investment courses and developed a website called Insight Investing (www.Insight-Investing.com). Although focused primarily on helping independent investors in the UK (where I am based), I will refer to it throughout the book as it contains useful templates that can be employed for analyzing investment opportunities wherever you are in the world.

Setting up my own business and taking control of my investments has enabled me to fulfill some of my dreams. Over the past few years I have been privileged enough to watch the sun rise on the Taj Mahal as it changed from deepest pink to dazzling white; to wake up in a floating Amazonian lodge to the cries of howler monkeys; and to climb a live volcano in Indonesia to sit on the edge of its crater as the first light of dawn crept across the Indian Ocean below. But here's the thing: for every dollar I've earned over the past decade, I now have a dollar sitting in investments.

Let me put this into context. Suppose you earn $100,000 a year for ten years, giving you total earnings of $1 million. One way to accumulate $1 million at the end of the decade would have been to live frugally and put every spare dollar under the mattress. Even doing this would inevitably mean ending up with less money than you earned; after all, you've got to eat. By contrast, imagine being able to enjoy a far more lavish lifestyle and still have $1 million left at the end of the ten years. That is what investing has done for me. Of course, there are no guarantees – investments can fall in value just as easily as they can increase. However, if you understand the rules of investing and how to apply them, you should be able to ensure that the gains you make will far outweigh any losses.

This book is a jargon-free, step-by-step guide to how to make your own investment decisions, based on sound commercial principles. But we're going to do more than that. We're going to find out how to make these decisions fast (you don't want to be spending several hours every week with your head buried in reports) and, just as importantly, how to keep the risk low (nobody wants to lose their money).

Just what do we mean by investing? In this book we're going to use the term to refer to any situation – not merely trading in shares – where you are parting with money now in the hope of achieving some sort of return (i.e., benefit) in the future. Although there are a wide variety of such opportunities, we will be confining our attention to those most accessible to the independent investor.

Running my own consultancy has provided me with the opportunity to meet and work with a wide variety of people who are all involved in making money grow. Probably the most important lesson I have learned from these encounters is that making a good investment decision is all about discipline: focusing your attention on the relevant facts and not allowing your judgment to be swayed by emotions. To achieve this, you need to adopt a structured approach to your investment decision-making. In this book I outline just such an approach, one that will enable you to maximize your potential gains while minimizing your potential losses; and an approach that will allow you to make investment decisions quickly, while ensuring that you have paid due consideration to risk and all other pertinent issues.

In addition to having a disciplined approach, if you want to make good investment decisions, it is essential that you know what your options are. Consequently, this is a book that is intended to be read in its entirety.

Chapter 1, Grow your own money, sets the scene, explaining why it's important to boost your wealth and how you can benefit by making your own investment decisions.

The next three chapters are dedicated to developing a structured approach that can be applied to any investment decision. Chapter 2, There are no experts, introduces the fundamental principles of investing, which are far more straightforward than is often made out, as well as explaining the concept of risk and the tradeoff between risk and reward. Chapter 3, The big four investment opportunities, explains that investing is about making choices and that there are four main opportunities available to the independent investor. Each has its own unique risk profile and we will discover how to make allowance for this when deciding which opportunities may be right for you. Chapter 4, The 6R approach to investing, is critical. While regrettably this approach to making investment decisions does not guarantee that every decision you make will be a winner – nothing can do that – it does provide a disciplined approach that you can apply to any investment opportunity: an approach that will help you maximize your returns while minimizing your risks.

Chapters 5 to 9 examine the big four investment opportunities in much more depth. We're not only concerned here with developing a sound understanding of how these investments work, we're also looking for fast and effective ways to assess potential opportunities. These chapters are all about learning the shortcuts, getting at the required information fast. That does not mean we're going to rush our decisions, simply that we're going to balance our use of time against the potential rewards.

Chapter 10, You can't win if you don't play, consolidates everything covered in the preceding chapters. It provides a practical, structured, and time-effective methodology for managing your investments.

To ease your progress through the book and enable you to review the content quickly, a few features have been incorporated within the text:

* Terms commonly encountered in the world of investing are highlighted in bold, accompanied by explanations of what each term means.
* "Quick challenges" invite you to stop and think about a question or decision.
* "Key measures" contain details of measures that can prove to be particularly useful when it comes to assessing investment opportunities.
* "Grow your own money" sections provide tips on how to become a more successful independent investor and how to simplify the decision-making process.

*   "The essentials" at the end of each chapter offer a
      handy summary of the main points.

Throughout the book monetary amounts are quoted
in dollars. Don't read too much into this: I've elected to
adopt the dollar simply because it's an instantly recogniz-
able international currency symbol. The point to note is
that the principles of investing are the same regardless of
where in the world you live.

Although this book is dedicated to helping you make
your own investment decisions, I am not saying that you
should never seek help. If you want to set up complex trusts
or intricate tax-efficient structures, professional advice may
well prove invaluable. In my experience, though, having
presented to many thousands of delegates over the years,
most everyday investment decisions are well within the
grasp of the average person. It is how to make these decisions that is the subject of this book.

1

GROW YOUR OWN MONEY

This is a book about money – your money – and how to make it grow. Whether you have a large or small amount of cash, with it comes a dilemma: What do you do with it? It is important that you make the right decisions, because what you do with your money today can have a dramatic impact on the lifestyle you enjoy in the future. Of course, you could keep your money under the mattress. However, if you actually want to grow your money, the only way you can do this is by investing it.

Investing is not difficult

The objective of investing is always the same: to start off with a pile of money (no matter how small) and to grow it into a larger pile. People understand the concept of working for money: you get a job, put in the hours, and in return receive an income from your employer – you are trading your time for money. In theory, if not necessarily always in practice, the more hours you work, the more money you will earn. Wouldn't it be nice if as well as you working for money, you got your money to work for you? That is what investing is all about: it makes your money work for you.

This book is dedicated to developing just one skill set, spotting a good investment and spotting a bad investment – nothing more, nothing less. If you can do that, you are on your way to a more prosperous future. The good news is you don't need to be a financial wizard to achieve this. Yes, we will need to address a few technicalities along the way, but rest assured, the financial rewards that these will open up for you will more than justify the occasional mild headache. As I often say in my presentations, "You don't need to be a world-class chef to prepare a great meal – you just need to be good at the basics."

Even though the principles are reasonably straight-forward, many people shy away from the world of invest-ing, for two common reasons:

* "I don't want to lose my money."
* "I don't have the time."

Both of these views are based on misconceptions, so let's lay them firmly to rest before going any further.

People are (quite rightly) fearful of losing some or all of their money and will therefore tend to avoid any activ-ity that they believe could put their money at risk. It is true that investing involves risk, but so does everything we do. Crossing the road involves risk. You might be struck by a vehicle and if this happened the consequences could be very serious indeed. Yet we are prepared to cross roads every day. By being aware of what the risks are, we are able to take action to minimize them. Even before we take the first step to cross the road, we will check visually to make sure there are no oncoming vehicles. We will also listen out for more distant traffic that may not yet be in view. We might endeavor to reduce risk further by using a pedestrian crossing. These actions do not remove the risk completely, but being aware of the risk has allowed us to take steps to minimize the threat.

So it is with investing. An important criterion for being a successful independent investor is being aware of the risks and, most importantly, being able to take appropriate action to mitigate them – being aware that risks can be managed.

What many people also fail to recognize is that it is the very existence of risk that creates opportunities. Suppose there is an investment that is guaranteed to pay you a 5% rate of return each year. The attraction is that it is risk free, but the downside is that you cannot earn more than 5%. Ironically, if the rate of return is not guaranteed, that is when the opportunity to earn more than 5% exists. If you want to be a successful independent investor, you have to learn how to embrace risk, not shy away from it.

Moving on to the time issue, investing does take time, but the point is this: Do the benefits justify the time? Given that investing is all about getting your money to work for you, if you have to commit a lot of time to making investment decisions, you've lost one of the incentives for investing in the first place.

QUICK CHALLENGE
How long would you be prepared to spend making a decision that could make you $1,000 in the next year?

If you could make $1,000 in the next year based on a decision that will take up half an hour of your time, you may feel that is worthy of consideration. But if you had to spend a whole month making that decision, you're not really investing at all; you've simply found another job, as you're still having to work for that money. You need to balance the potential rewards against the time it takes to make the decision. As a general principle, the money you

earn from each hour dedicated to making investment decisions should far outweigh the money you would make if
you were to spend the same time doing a regular job.

So yes, investing does involve an element of risk, but
the risks can be managed. And yes, decisions do take time
to make, but the benefits should more than compensate
for any hours you put in.

Being an independent investor

When making investment decisions, like many tasks
in life, there are two possible approaches:

* . DIY (doing it yourself).
* GSI (getting someone in).

It's a little like wanting to paint your living room. The
problem with doing it yourself is that it's time consuming and maybe you're also dubious about your decorating
skills. The problem with getting someone in, of course, is
that they're going to charge you for their services.

Suppose you do opt for the GSI approach. You need to
be pretty convinced on two issues: first, that they're going
to save you a lot of time; and secondly, that they're going
to do a good job. Investing is not too different. Should you
do it yourself or should you get someone in? However, it's
at this stage that the similarities end.

So you contact a decorator with the intention of giving your living room a fresh new look, and find that there's
a fixed fee for the work, payable in advance. The decorator
insists on deciding the color scheme, what paint to buy,
and what materials to use. Your living room may end up
looking better, or it may end up looking considerably worse

than it is now; either way, you must pay the fee. How do you feel about the proposal? That is the deal you're being offered when you pay someone else to invest your money for you. They are going to charge you regardless of whether they do a good job or not. Call me old-fashioned, but I regard that as a complete non-starter. Can you think of any other industry that charges you for goods and services regardless of whether you get what you want? And what is particularly worrying is that the financial services sector is very accomplished at making its services seem good value.

QUICK CHALLENGE
You have $100,000 that you want to invest to build up a nest egg over the next 20 years. How much would you be prepared to pay for some help in investing it?

If you use the services of a financial adviser, they are going to charge you a fee for their services, maybe 1% of the fund value. In this example that's $1,000, which doesn't sound too bad, does it? It is highly likely the adviser will in turn place the money with a fund manager, who will also charge a fee. Their annual management charge might be a further 1% of the sum invested. In addition, the fund will be subject to administration charges, such as the costs of buying and selling shares, and these may add up to another 0.5% of the fund value. So the total charge to manage your investment in this instance works out at $2,500. Yes, it's quite a lot, but given that you're investing $100,000, maybe it's not so bad.

Now comes the twist: it's $2,500 every year. That means you can expect to pay out $50,000 over the next 20 years, so half of the amount you have available to invest right now is going to disappear in fees. It could end up

considerably more than this if the fund has been growing, bearing in mind that the fees are based on the value
of the fund. That is the cost of getting someone in. If you
are going to spend that sort of money, you have got to be
pretty certain you would not prefer to do it yourself.

This highlights a key advantage of being an independent investor: it can save you a fortune in fees. The other
advantage is that it puts you in control: you decide where
your money is going to go.

Refusing to invest is not an option

Before progressing any further, let's rule out one strategy you should never adopt. Many people avoid the world
of investing because they are fearful they might lose some
or all of their money, but then go on to pursue the one
course of action that is guaranteed to do just that: they do
nothing. But how can doing nothing lose you money?

It is time to introduce one of the greatest enemies of
your hard-earned cash. **Inflation** refers to the increasing
prices of goods and services: as time goes by, prices go
up. It is a sad fact of life that inflation is present in most
economies around the globe. This is why you should never
leave money under a mattress, in a coffee jar, or in whatever other storage device you might care to employ.

Suppose you have $2,000 in cash right now, which is
enough to buy that television system you have craved with
full surround sound. But you're not sure you can justify
the expenditure, so you store the money in a box under
your bed for the next year, during which time the price
of that dream television system has gone up by 5%. In a
year's time you still have $2,000, but that television system
would now cost you $2,100 and you can no longer afford

it. By refusing to invest, you end up financially worse off
than you are now. What this tells us is that even if you simply want to preserve the purchasing power of the cash you
currently possess, you have no real choice but to invest it.

THE ESSENTIALS

* **Investing is not difficult – to be a successful independent investor, you just need to be good at the basics.**
* **You can manage risk – being aware of what the risks are enables you to take steps to mitigate them.**
* **Investing need not be time consuming – the potential rewards should more than compensate for the limited amount of time you need to spend making the decisions in the first place.**
* **Don't be afraid to make your own investment decisions – it puts you in control and can save you a fortune in fees.**
* **Refusing to invest is not an option – inflation will eat away at the purchasing power of your hard-earned cash.**

2

THERE ARE NO EXPERTS

The world of finance seems to be in the news on a daily basis. "The Dow Jones rallied this morning" and "The banking crisis is deepening" are not merely interesting events: whether directly or indirectly, they have an impact on your financial wellbeing. They affect the value of your home, your investments, and even your pension. Not surprisingly, you may feel as if you're on a financial roller-coaster: you want to take control, you want to invest your money, but who can you trust?

Nobody cares more about your money than you do

Stories about banking scandals, casino mentality fund managers, mis-selling scandals, bogus investment schemes, and rogue traders have simply reinforced the view that the so-called professionals can be far more motivated by personal gain than by the performance of your investments. Indeed, the credit crunch and its aftermath are testimony to the fact that there are no experts: nobody knows for certain what the future holds. Although there are many explanations for the origins of the credit crunch, and many books have been written on the topic, the true problem was remarkably basic. Financial institutions were making horrendous investment decisions. They were lending money that was unlikely ever to be repaid, they were investing in businesses that subsequently failed, and they bought financial instruments that they did not even understand. These investment decisions were so catastrophic that they almost brought the global economy to its knees.

These so-called experts were ignoring a fundamental principle of investing: the tradeoff between risk and reward. Investments with little risk tend to offer low returns, while it is the higher-risk investments that typically offer potentially higher rates of return. This is basic stuff and any prospective investor should be aware of, and most importantly respect, this principle, yet for years it had been blatantly ignored. Financial institutions were pursuing higher returns and ignoring the risks.

A key issue underpinning all investment decisions is trust. Who do you trust with your money? What the credit crunch has taught us is that if you are going to hand your money over to a third party, you need to be reasonably confident that they have your interests at heart. There is a big difference between an organization that wants to make money for you and an organization that wants to make money out of you. As an independent investor, I firmly hold to my mantra: "Nobody cares more about your money than you do!" I now make all my own investment decisions and I genuinely believe that I am far better off financially as a result. Even ignoring how my investments are performing, the savings in fees have been substantial.

Your first decision

If you aspire to be a successful independent investor, you have to appreciate that when you have money, you have three options regarding what to do with it. You can spend it on day-to-day goods and services, going for meals out, and taking holidays. The alternative is to tie up your money in **assets** (that simply means things you own), which then presents two further options. You can spend it on depreciating assets, things you own that lose value over time, such as a television or a car. Alternatively, you can invest it in wealth-creating assets, things you own that can enhance your wealth by increasing in value and/or providing an income. For example, property can both increase in value and generate rental income.

It's time for a quick point of clarification. As soon as people hear the word wealth, they invariably think about mansions, yachts, and private jets. Being wealthy is not the same as having wealth. Most people have some wealth, which may be a lot or it may be a little. Wealth simply means things you own. Whether you own a lot or a little, you have wealth. When we talk about growing your own money we're simply talking about increasing your wealth – starting with a pile of money (your current wealth) and creating a larger pile of money in the future (your future wealth).

It is important to be aware of the implications of choosing each of the three options being presented to you. If you spend $100 on goods and services today, you will receive $100 worth of goods and services today. This will result in your wealth decreasing. This is called consumption: your money is being spent on things you will consume. That does not mean that spending money on day-to-day goods and services is a bad thing, but just bear in mind that every dollar being spent on goods and services is a dollar that could have been invested to increase your future wealth.

Depreciating assets are different. If you spend $100 today, you will acquire $100 worth of assets that could

Spend it on goods ← **What should I do** → **Spend it on**
and services   **with my money?**   **depreciating assets**

Invest it in
wealth-creating assets

MONEY PRESENTS CHOICES

provide benefits over several years. Spending $2,000 on
a television system should provide you with many years
of viewing pleasure. As time progresses, though, the system will lose value, so just like goods and services, this
form of expenditure will ultimately result in your wealth
decreasing. The key difference in this instance is you will
lose wealth at a slower rate.

That leaves one option. If you want to increase your
wealth, you have no alternative but to invest it in wealth-
creating assets. Pursuing this course of action means that
investing $100 today could result in you receiving back sig-
nificantly more than $100 in the future.

Take Adam and Harry. Each of them earns $50,000 a
year and they both work for 40 years. Adam spends everything as he earns it, so that during his working life he is
able to spend $2 million. By contrast, Harry invests some
of his income each year, so that during his working life
he manages to create additional wealth of $2 million.

Consequently, he is able to spend $4 million. These are two ordinary guys with similar jobs, yet Harry enjoys the more lavish lifestyle. What makes Harry different is that he does not only go to work for money; he also makes his money work for him.

Welcome to your wealth

Having established your basic options for what you can do with money, if you want to start off with a pile of money and end up with a larger pile of money, the next logical step is to determine how much you are worth at the outset. Most people know how much they earn, but surprisingly few know how much they are worth.

You can determine what you are worth right now by preparing a document known as a **balance sheet**, which is simply a statement of wealth. This is a straightforward exercise. You start by adding up everything you own – your assets. Now, if you did not owe anybody any money, that would be your wealth. Unfortunately, most people also have debts and the amounts you owe are called **liabilities**. Therefore, to establish your wealth, you need to deduct all of your liabilities from your assets. Whatever is left over is called your net assets, which is just another term for wealth.

In case you are wondering, the reason it is called a balance sheet is because it comprises a list of balances, another word for values. It lists the balances (values) of your assets and it lists the balances (values) of your liabilities – mystery solved.

Opposite is an example of a personal balance sheet for Len Dussmore.

LEN DUSSMORE

WHAT DO I OWN?		$
	Wealth-creating assets	400,000
	Depreciating assets	100,000
	Total assets	500,000

WHAT DO I OWE?		
	Total liabilities	350,000

WHAT IS MY CURRENT WEALTH?		
	Net assets	150,000

BALANCE SHEET

In order to calculate his wealth, Len starts off by listing everything he owns: his assets. Whether or not he has borrowed money to acquire these assets is irrelevant; the point is that they are his. If Len's house is worth $300,000 but he owes $240,000 on the mortgage, the truth of the matter is that he owns a house that is worth $300,000 and that should be included in the list. The mortgage will be accounted for in the liabilities section of the document. In this instance Len has established that he has assets worth $500,000, of which $400,000 worth are wealth creating and as such could potentially increase his future financial wellbeing. This latter figure would include items such as savings accounts, company shares, pension funds, and property. The other $100,000 worth are depreciating assets, which would typically include things like cars, furniture, equipment, and clothing; these are losing value. This already sets Len a challenge. Just to maintain his current financial status he needs to ensure that the additional wealth being created by his wealth-creating assets at least matches the wealth being lost in his depreciating assets. Failing to do this means that his overall wealth will ultimately decrease – the exact opposite of what he wants to achieve.

Having written down everything he owns, Len then adds up everything he owes (his liabilities). For many people this is the frightening bit! Typical liabilities would include mortgages, car loans, credit card bills, taxes owing, and so on. In this instance we can see that Len owes $350,000.

When constructing a balance sheet for yourself, you don't have to be 100% accurate with all the numbers; approximations will do. All you are trying to do is get a feel for what you are worth right now. In Len's case, with assets of $500,000 and liabilities of $350,000, we can see that he has net assets of $150,000. What this calculation tells us is that if Len sold everything he owned and paid off everything he owed, he would still have $150,000 left – this is his current wealth.

When constructing a balance sheet for the first time, it will take a little time and I agree it probably will not provide the same adrenalin rush as skydiving or power-boat racing. However, constructing a balance sheet will move you one step closer to enhancing your wealth, and that certainly ought to maintain your interest. This document won't simply tell you how much you are worth right now

– it will also provide a means of monitoring your progress in the future.

GROW YOUR OWN MONEY
Preparing a balance sheet once a year is a great way to assess the effectiveness of your money-growing skills.

There is a tradeoff
between risk and reward

Having successfully constructed a balance sheet, if you aspire to be a successful independent investor you next need to understand the tradeoff between risk and reward.

You have some money, but you just don't know what to do with it. Maybe you should put it in a savings account and earn some interest; that is a safe option. You've heard talk of corporate bonds, but you don't really understand how they work. A couple of colleagues at work claim there's never been a better time to invest in the stock market. Property is another option; maybe you should invest in a holiday home. Then there's your retirement to think about: you want to make sure you have enough set aside for that. With so many options, how can you ever hope to make a sensible decision?

The concept of the **rate of return** looks at the annual benefit derived from an investment as a percentage of the amount invested – this is your reward.

QUICK CHALLENGE
Offer 1
If someone asked you to give them $1,000 now and promised to give you back $1,010 in one year's time, would you accept?

Offer 2
If that same person asked you to give them $1,000 now and promised to give you back $1,500 in one year's time, would you accept?

If you're like most people, you would probably reject the first offer but accept the second one. The reason for the differing responses is at the heart of wealth creation. In the first scenario you may feel that the reward is inadequate to compensate for sacrificing access to your cash, whereas in the second scenario you may well feel that the sacrifice is worthwhile. What you are looking at, albeit subconsciously, is the rate of return. The first scenario is only offering a 1% rate of return ($10 annual benefit as a percentage of your $1,000 investment), whereas the second scenario offers a rate of return of 50% ($500 annual benefit as a percentage of your $1,000 investment).

Deciding if you should spend money (whether it be on day-to-day goods and services or depreciating assets, or if you should invest it in wealth-creating assets) is all about answering a question: Would you prefer a sandwich today or a banquet tomorrow? This principle is at the very heart of investing: weighing up the sacrifice now against the perceived future benefit.

This is the first discipline when it comes to making any investment decision. Whenever you are considering an investment opportunity, at the outset you must ask yourself this question: What rate of return can I achieve by sacrificing money now? I am aghast at how many people I have met who have parted with their money without having a clue as to the rate of return they are likely to achieve.

Based on the discussion so far, it may well appear that investing is all about seeking out those opportunities that offer the highest rate of return. In practice, though, seasoned investors rarely do this. Why not? Because, when you look at rate of return, what you are actually looking at is the *potential* rate of return. When you invest money, you are parting with cash now in the hope of achieving a decent rate of return in the future. The problem is, because you are dealing in the future, no rate of return can be guaranteed, which means that, through the mere act of investing, you are entering the world of **risk**.

Most people's understanding of risk is that it concerns the possibility of something going wrong. The most fundamental thing that can go wrong here is that the investment loses value – you get back less than you invested – which is many people's greatest fear. So, in order to entice you into higher-risk investments, the potential rates of return have to increase. Not surprisingly, then, there tends to be a tradeoff between risk and rate of return: the higher the rate of return you want to achieve, the more risk you must be prepared to accept. Consequently, when it comes to identifying which types of wealth-creating asset are right for you, not only should you look at the potential reward, you also need to look at the associated risk.

The good news is that risk can be managed; it is just a skill set you need to develop. Imagine that you are baking a cake and you have no cooking experience. You are surrounded by ingredients laid out in a stunning array of colors and producing wonderful aromas. The trouble is that you have no idea what any of them are. All you can do is mix up some of them and hope for the best. In this situation the chances of producing something remotely edible will be very low – it is all risk – but if you dedicate time to learning about some of the ingredients, the chances of success increase. The more you know about the ingredients, the more confident you will become.

Having knowledge about the investments you intend to make has two distinct advantages:

* You are able to exploit potential gains.
* You are better placed to minimize losses.

It follows that the more risky the investment, the more knowledge you will need to develop. Of course, it would be unrealistic to expect every investment decision you ever make to be a good one. The objective of developing knowledge is to ensure that any occasional losses you do make will be more than adequately outweighed by your gains. That approach has certainly worked for me. Indeed, I always view any poor investment decision as a valuable learning opportunity. I review the circumstances that led up to the original decision and identify what I could do differently in the future to avoid making the same mistake again.

Risk is not the only consideration

You will encounter many investors who believe that investing is all about managing the tradeoff between risk and reward, but the problem is not quite that straightforward.

Suppose you buy shares in a company for $1,000 and six months later they have dropped in value to $900, but two years after that they have increased to $1,500. If you sold them after six months, you would indeed make a loss, but if you sold them after two years you would make a profit. This explains why people are prepared to invest in shares. Although the value of their investment might fall in the short term, they expect it to increase in the long term.

What this tells us is that the tradeoff between risk and rate of return is not quite as clear cut as you might expect. If you intend to invest in shares for just a few months, they are indeed high risk and there is a very real possibility that you could end up with less money than you started with. By contrast, if you are prepared to invest money for several years, the risk of losing money is greatly diminished. What we have just established is that risk is affected by **term**, the period of time for which you are prepared to tie up your cash. It follows that both risk and term are relevant when making any investment decision, but there are other considerations too.

Not being able to access your cash when you need it is, for many people, the worst situation to be in. This is a powerful motive for keeping money in a bank account or an instant access savings account, as you can get at your cash whenever you need it. If it is likely you may need access to cash at short notice, **liquidity** suddenly becomes important (liquidity simply means having ready access to cash). This is another consideration that must be addressed when confronted with an investment opportunity.

There is one other issue you need to consider: **capital**, the amount you have to invest at the outset. Savings accounts demand very little capital – some can be opened with as little as $1, whereas, by contrast, property often demands capital running into hundreds of thousands or even millions of dollars.

You can improve returns without increasing risk

Although liquidity, term, and capital are relevant, the most critical tradeoff in most investors' minds is still the tradeoff between risk and reward: the greater the risk you are prepared to assume, the higher your potential rate of return.

It's time for some financial wizardry! There is a principle that allows you to improve your returns without assuming any additional risk, called **compounding**. In the world of investing, compounding refers to the reinvestment of income, and it can have a dramatic impact on your wealth-creating ability.

When you make money on any investment, you have two options as to what you can do with the proceeds: you can spend them or you can reinvest them. Suppose at the age of 20 you invest $30,000 for 40 years, on which you achieve an annual rate of return of 10%. If you withdrew the income each year, you would be earning $3,000 per annum, which over the next 40 years would add up to $120,000. Don't forget that you will also get back your original investment of $30,000. That means you will have turned a $30,000 investment into $150,000 over a 40-year timespan – not bad. Now suppose that instead of withdrawing the income each year, you reinvest it at 10% per annum. Let's see how this would affect performance.

As previously, you invest $30,000 at the age of 20 for 40 years and once again you achieve an annual rate of return of 10%. At the end of the first year you will have $33,000, comprising the original investment of $30,000 plus $3,000 income. If you decide to reinvest that income, you will be investing $33,000 at the start of the second year, on which you will earn 10% over the next 12 months. So at the end of the second year you will have $36,300, comprising the $33,000 investment plus $3,300 income. Once again, you reinvest all the income, which means you will be starting off the third year with $36,300 invested on which you will earn 10%, so at the end of the third year you will have $39,930, comprising the $36,300 investment plus $3,630 income. This will continue in the ensuing years. Pursuing this strategy means you would receive no income over the next 40 years, but at the age of 60 you would be sitting on $1,357,777. Instead of turning $30,000 into $150,000, you would have managed to turn the same $30,000 into over $1.3 million and you would have achieved this without taking on any additional risk. All you have to do is reinvest your income – that is the power of compounding. You see, becoming a millionaire really isn't that difficult; the challenge is being able to find an investment that will deliver that 10% annual rate of return.

Investing has two great friends – rate of return and time – and compounding brings these two concepts together. To appreciate its power fully, we are going to revisit your $30,000 investment, earning 10% per annum. The table below compares what happens to its value over time if you do not reinvest your income with what happens if you do.

INVESTING $30,000 EARNING 10% INCOME PER ANNUM

Investment period	Total received back if income is not reinvested	Total received back if income is reinvested
10 years	$60,000	$77,812
20 years	$90,000	$201,824
30 years	$120,000	$523,482
40 years	$150,000	$1,357,777

THE IMPACT OF TIME ON COMPOUNDING

What this table demonstrates is that in addition to improving your overall return, compounding also produces a more subtle phenomenon. If you withdraw your income each year, after 10 years you will make a profit of $30,000 (the $60,000 you receive back less the $30,000 original investment). If you can wait 20 years, your profit increases to $60,000 (the $90,000 you receive back less the $30,000 original investment). In other words, if you withdraw income each year, doubling your investment period from 10 to 20 years will double your profit, which for many people is what they would expect. That is not what happens if you are prepared to reinvest your income each year.

If you do reinvest your income, after 10 years you will make a profit of $47,812 (the $77,812 you receive back less the $30,000 original investment), but after 20 years your profit increases to $171,824 (the $201,824 you receive back less the $30,000 original investment). By doubling your investment horizon, your profit has increased by 260%. The longer the time you invest your money for, the more pronounced this effect becomes. If you are prepared to invest your money for 40 years, the profit increases to $1,327,777 (the $1,357,777 you receive back less the $30,000 original investment). So doubling the investment period from 20 years to 40 years increases the profit from $171,824 to $1,327,777 – an increase of over 670%.

This is an important feature of compounding: double the length of time you invest money for and you will more than double your profit; the longer you can invest for, the more spectacular your returns can become. Whether you are earning 5% or 50% return on your investment each year, this basic principle holds true.

GROW YOUR OWN MONEY
To maximize your returns, reinvest your income.

So according to the compounding principle, the amount of money you end up with will be determined by three factors:

* The value of the original investment.
* The annual rate of return you achieve on your investment.
* How long you invest your money for.

Increasing any of these components can enhance your future wealth.

THE ESSENTIALS
* **Construct a personal balance sheet – this will tell you your current wealth and can be used to monitor how your wealth is growing in years to come.**
* **Check the rate of return – when looking at any investment opportunity, always confirm the potential rate of return.**
* **Consider liquidity, risk, term, and capital – they all affect the appeal of an investment opportunity.**
* **Don't forget compounding – reinvesting income can dramatically enhance the amount of money you end up with.**

3

THE BIG FOUR INVESTMENT
OPPORTUNITIES

I f you want to grow your money, you have no choice but to invest it in wealth-creating assets that can be expected to generate an income and/or increase in value in the future. Although there are many types of asset that provide this opportunity – fine wine, art, and gold, for example – these are specialist areas and should only be ventured into by those well versed in these particular markets. Lower-risk initiatives such as peer-to-peer lending have also gained in popularity, but even these should be approached with a certain amount of caution. Consequently, most investors (whether independent investors or major financial institutions) tend to confine their attention to just four opportunities. Colloquially known as the "big four," they comprise savings accounts (i.e., cash deposits), bonds, shares (or stocks), and property. This means, in order to take control of your own investment decisions, you need to understand just four markets.

Your first problem is to determine which of the "big four" are right for you. Let us start by looking at the main features of each type of investment.

Savings accounts

. When it comes to savings there are many types of account available, but they all tend to work the same way.

Savings accounts

Bonds

Shares

Property

Where should I invest?

FOUR MAIN TYPES OF WEALTH-CREATING ASSET

In essence, when you open a **savings account**, you are lending money to a financial institution. In return for the use of your funds, the institution undertakes to pay interest while it has access to your money and to repay the loan in full. The benefit to you is the opportunity to earn interest. Against this you must evaluate what you are sacrificing in terms of liquidity, risk, term, and capital.

For many investors, liquidity is the most critical issue governing their investment decisions – having access to cash when they need it. This can make savings accounts appear particularly attractive as many offer immediate access to your funds, although sometimes you may incur a penalty if you fail to give adequate notice of a proposed withdrawal.

When it comes to risk, although savings accounts are commonly regarded as low risk, they are not risk free; financial institutions can fail. If you select your financial institution carefully, though, the likelihood of losing some or all of your investment is remote.

As far as term is concerned, savings accounts tend to earn interest from the moment funds are deposited, so you can expect to achieve a return even if you only invest for a few days.

Finally, when it comes to capital, some savings accounts can be opened with as little as one dollar.

In order to achieve these benefits, savers are prepared to accept lower rates of return than are available on other types of investment. Consequently, savings accounts tend to be regarded more as a means of protecting funds against inflation than as a practical way of increasing wealth. It is highly unlikely you will meet anyone who has made their millions by putting money in a savings account!

The following table summarizes the key features of savings accounts in terms of potential rates of return and the associated tradeoffs, where a tick ($\checkmark$) indicates that the issue is not usually significant while a cross ($\times$) denotes that the issue is always significant.

	SAVINGS ACCOUNTS	
Return	Low	Savings accounts tend to be used to protect funds against inflation.
Liquidity	$\checkmark$	Many accounts offer immediate access to funds.
Risk	$\checkmark$	If deposited with reputable institutions, it is unlikely you will lose any of your investment.
Term	$\checkmark$	Interest tends to be earned from the day funds are deposited.
Capital	$\checkmark$	Accounts can be opened with as little as $1.

THE KEY FEATURES OF SAVINGS ACCOUNTS

Bonds

If you want to achieve higher rates of return but without a significant increase in risk, **bonds** may offer a solution. They tend to offer more favorable rates of return than savings accounts, while at the same time being less risky than shares, yet very few independent investors understand what bonds are or how they work.

Governments (both national and local) often need to borrow money, as do companies. The amounts involved can be substantial and this in itself can create a problem. Suppose a company needs to borrow $500 million for the next 20 years. One way to raise the funds would be to negotiate a straightforward loan, but there are few organizations that would be willing to consider lending such a substantial sum for that length of time. An alternative approach is to break up the loan into individual bonds of (say) $1,000 each. A bond is a tradable instrument whereby the organization that is trying to raise the finance promises to pay the bearer interest over a predetermined period of time, with repayment of the full amount borrowed taking place at the end of the term. Furthermore, because organizations like to be able to plan their financial commitments, it is common practice to fix the rate of interest payable at the outset. As a result, bonds are often referred to as fixed income securities.

Suppose you subscribe for some $1,000 bonds issued by MT Pokkits, which are paying 5% a year and which will be repayable on December 31, 2026. The point to bear in mind is bonds are tradable: they can be bought and sold. This is good news for you. If you need access to cash, you can sell the bonds at any time to another investor who will in effect be taking over the loan. This means that bonds offer two potential benefits:

* They can provide a regular income in the form of interest.
* They can provide a **capital gain** (a term commonly used to refer to the increase in value of an investment).

This latter point needs explanation. Just as house prices can vary, so too can bond prices. The price you will achieve for each bond you sell may be more or less than $1,000, depending on the amount that prospective buyers are prepared to pay on the day.

Many investors are attracted to bonds purely because they can provide a higher rate of interest than savings accounts. If you want to keep risk reasonably low, which is a strategy I endorse throughout the book, this is the approach to adopt. Another strategy that is far higher risk endeavors to exploit the volatility in bond prices and involves buying bonds in the hope that prices will go up in the future, so that they can subsequently be sold for a profit. This is pure speculation and should not be regarded as an effective means of wealth creation.

Let's look at the key features of this type of investment, starting with liquidity. Given that bonds are tradable, they can be sold whenever the need arises. Bear in mind, though, that depending on when you sell them, you may receive back more or less than you paid for them.

As far as risk is concerned, the primary concern is default: the issuer failing to maintain interest payments and/or failing to repay the loan. Depending on the issuer, bonds can range from very low to very high risk. For example, bonds issued by governments of some of the world's leading economies are regarded as one of the safest forms of investment available (even safer than savings accounts), while those issued by struggling companies may be viewed as far riskier. By restricting attention to low-risk government and company bonds, the likelihood of your losing some or all of your investment can be kept to a minimum.

When it comes to term, bonds are available that promise to pay a guaranteed rate of interest for a variety of terms ranging from a few days to 30 years or more. As a general principle, the longer the term until redemption, the higher the rate of interest that will be on offer. Not surprisingly, then, most investors tend to view bonds as an investment to generate income over a period of years, rather than days.

Finally, there is the capital commitment. Often bond issues require a minimum purchase value, $1,000 or more not being unusual.

	BONDS	
Return	Medium	Bonds can offer higher rates of return than savings accounts.
Liquidity	✔	Bonds can be sold as required, although you may incur a loss in doing so.
Risk	✔	Careful selection of bonds can keep risk low.
Term	✕	Bonds tend to be regarded as an investment that spans years rather than months.
Capital	✕	A minimum investment of at least $1,000 is not unusual.

THE KEY FEATURES OF BONDS

Shares

Whether you put your money into savings accounts or into bonds, you are entering into a loan arrangement with a government, financial institution, or trading company. In most cases your money will be reasonably secure, although there is still an element of risk, so rates of return do not tend to be particularly spectacular. If you are looking to grow your money significantly in the future, you need to cast your attention elsewhere.

There are two main types of wealth-creating asset that create such an opportunity: shares and property.

Shares are usually perceived as the most intricate form of investment, though in fact the principles underpinning them really are quite straightforward. And television footage of trading rooms with people jumping up and down and screaming hysterically over desks, while video screens in the background display a seemingly endless stream of figures, does nothing to help allay the fear that exists in people's minds. In fact, if you want to be successful at investing in shares, jumping up and down and screaming hysterically is the last thing you ought to be doing. The very nature of shares suggests that the most effective way to earn money is to be calm and relaxed when making your decisions.

Let's be clear about what a share is. In order to trade, companies typically need to raise funds from investors, but in the majority of cases it is unlikely they will be able to raise all the money they need from only one individual. To address this issue, companies issue shares, representing part ownership of the business. If a company issues one million shares and you happen to own one of them, you own one millionth of the company; if you own

250,000 shares, you own a quarter of the company; if you own 500,000 shares, you own half of the company; and so on. Shares are also sometimes referred to as the stock or equity of a company, so when you hear people talking about stockholders or equity holders in a business, they are simply referring to the shareholders.

But what exactly do you own when you buy shares? First of all, you own a share of the assets. If you buy 10% of a company's shares and the company owns a factory worth $10 million, you (in theory at least) own 10% of that building. More importantly, you also own a right to a 10% share of all the company's future profits. Past profits have been and gone; what you are buying into is a slice of the future. This is what drives share prices: if a company is expected to be highly profitable in the future its shares will command a high share price, whereas if there are significant doubts about future profit performance the price will be much lower.

Like bonds, shares offer two potential benefits:

* They can provide a regular income if the company pays a **dividend** (a distribution of profit to the shareholders, typically paid out every few months).
* They can also provide a capital gain if they increase in value.

Your overall return is the combination of these two factors. If you buy a share for $100 and during the ensuing year you receive a dividend of $5, plus the value of the share increases by $15 up to $115, you have made a $20 return on a $100 investment.

Now we come to the issue that distinguishes shares from savings accounts and bonds. It is also the issue that deters many people from investing in shares in the first place. In the case of both savings accounts and bonds, you know in advance what your returns are going to be, whereas in the case of shares you do not. Although to the uninitiated this might seem to be a good reason not to invest in shares, it is the very fact that the future returns are not known that provides their big attraction. If you think about it, this means that there is no limit to the returns you might enjoy.

It is possible to make spectacular returns on a very small investment, provided that you manage to identify the appropriate opportunity. I have seen some of my shareholdings double or even treble in value in a matter of months, although regrettably this has tended to be the exception rather than the rule. There have also been some shares that have fallen in value, but that does not worry me. When it comes to investing in shares, it is common practice to build up a portfolio of several shares. The intention is not to find shares that will only increase in value (I've never met anyone yet who's managed to do this). The intention is to ensure that the gains you achieve are far greater than any losses you might incur. As long as you are able to do this, you will enjoy a healthy return on your overall investment.

The main challenge with shares is that nobody knows for sure what is going to happen in the future and expectations are continually changing. This explains why share prices are so volatile. This volatility gives rise to two types of participant in this market:

✳   Share traders.
✳   Share investors.

A trader regularly buys and sells shares in the hope of making money out of short-term fluctuations in the market. Day trading is the term commonly assigned to this activity. It offers high potential returns but is also high risk, particularly for the uninitiated. It is one thing to expect share prices to rise over the next year or two; it is a different thing entirely to guess what is going to happen to prices in the next few hours! Although rewards can be high, losses can be astronomical – this really is gambling on a grand scale, borne out by news stories of experienced traders working for major financial institutions losing billions of dollars, mind-boggling amounts of money. If these are the banks' experts, I would hate to meet the trainees.

A share investor takes a longer-term view, looking for companies that can provide returns significantly better than those offered by savings accounts and bonds, while accepting that this may not be achievable for at least two to three years. This can provide two potential benefits. Numerous studies have shown that the rates of return achieved on shares over a number of years will consistently outstrip those available on savings accounts and bonds; the evidence is overwhelming. In addition, it will put you in a position where (to a large degree) you can ignore short-term volatility in share prices, resulting in a more relaxed approach to life, coupled with an optimism that will enrich the lives of your friends and family!

Although shares can appear very attractive in terms of improved rates of return, we need to assess this in the light of liquidity, risk, term, and capital. Just like bonds, shares can be sold whenever the need arises, but share prices can go down as well as up and dividends are not guaranteed. So although shares generally enjoy good liquidity, there is also risk involved. As far as the term issue is concerned, due to short-term volatility, shares should be regarded as a medium- to long-term investment, covering at least two to three years (ideally longer). And what about capital? You usually pay a trading fee when you buy shares and you pay another fee when you sell them. To minimize the impact of these fees, you should normally expect to invest a minimum of $1,000 per company. Furthermore, most investors advocate having holdings in several companies, in order to reduce risk; putting all your eggs in one basket is deemed a high-risk strategy. To address this problem, you ideally ought to be starting off with a few thousand dollars.

	SHARES	
Return	High	Shares can offer high rates of return.
Liquidity	✔	Shares can be sold as required, although you may incur a loss in doing so.
Risk	✕	Share values can go down as well as up and dividends are not guaranteed.
Term	✕	Shares should be viewed as an investment that spans years rather than months.
Capital	✕	A minimum investment of $1,000 per transaction is typically required, plus having several holdings is usual.

THE KEY FEATURES OF SHARES

Property

While shares offer an opportunity to improve your wealth significantly in the long term, property offers an opportunity to increase your wealth at an even faster rate. Like both bonds and shares, property offers two potential benefits:

*   A capital gain can be achieved should the value of the property increase.
*   Income can be generated if the property is rented out.

This has given rise to three different types of property investor:

*   Property traders.
*   Property developers.
*   Landlords.

A trader makes money by simply buying and selling properties, securing properties below their market value (for example, where a quick sale is required) in the hope of subsequently selling them at a higher price. A developer makes money by enhancing property, either looking for plots of land on which to build new properties or for properties in need of restoration or further development. The intention is to carry out the necessary work and then sell the properties for a profit. Then there is the landlord, who is not in the business of buying and selling properties, but wants properties that will provide a reliable source of rental income.

The existence of traders, developers, and landlords has resulted in two very different approaches to property investing:

*   Buy to sell.
*   Buy to rent.

Property traders and property developers both adopt a buy to sell approach, whereas landlords take a buy to rent approach.

Inevitably, if high potential rates of return are on offer, sacrifices have to be made. Property is the most illiquid of the big four investment opportunities. It can take months (sometimes even longer) to dispose of a property. Experience has also shown time and time again that the value of property can go down as well as up, so there is risk involved. In addition, rental income can never be guaranteed. When it comes to term, it may be months or even years before you realize a return on your investment. However, the real differential when it comes to property compared to the other main types of wealth-creating assets is the capital required. Properties often cost hundreds of thousands or even millions of dollars. You really need to be sure you know what you're doing before you part with your cash.

	PROPERTY	
Return	Very high	Property can offer very high rates of return.
Liquidity	✕	Property can take months to sell.
Risk	✕	Property values can go down as well as up and rents are never guaranteed.
Term	✕	Buy to sell strategies can take months to execute; buy to rent is a far longer-term strategy.
Capital	✕	Properties can cost hundreds of thousands or millions of dollars.

THE KEY FEATURES OF PROPERTY

The big four compared

Of course, it is down to you to decide which of the four main types of wealth-creating asset are most appropriate to your circumstances and this will be influenced by the key features on offer. Although there are other pertinent issues, for the majority of investors the most critical issue when it comes to selecting appropriate investments is the tradeoff between risk and reward (i.e., the rate of return).

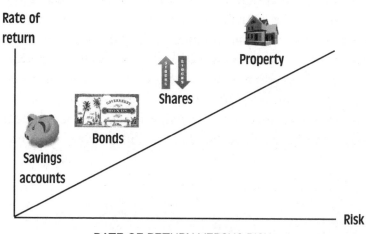

RATE OF RETURN VERSUS RISK

Savings accounts tend to be regarded as reasonably secure and therefore are usually viewed as a low-risk investment. There is little chance of your investment losing value unless the financial institution fails, so rates of return tend to be low. Bonds can offer higher rates of return, but bond prices can vary and there is always the possibility of the issuer defaulting, so the risk can still be low (if you choose your bonds carefully), but slightly higher than savings accounts. Share prices can be very volatile but, despite the increased volatility, it is unlikely that you will lose all of your money. Shares therefore tend to be associated with more risk than bonds, but also offer the prospect of higher returns. Finally, property prices can fall as well as rise. The big problem with property is that a considerable sum of money is often being tied up in a single asset. If that specific asset loses value, there is the potential to lose a lot of money very quickly, so property tends to be the most risky of all the wealth-creating assets; against this is the potential to achieve spectacular returns.

Insight Investing is home to the Insight Independent Investors Index, which tracks the performance of the big four investment opportunities in the UK and provides a summary of returns being achieved in each of the individual markets. If you do not live in the UK, periodically constructing a table similar to the one shown for your own country would provide an effective overview of the main investment opportunities available to you as an independent investor.

Insight Independent Investors Index					
As at 28th February 2014					
	CURRENT VALUE		YEAR TO DATE PERFORMANCE		
Savings	Index	1,001.2	Income	0.1%	More on Savings
	YTD change	+0.1%			
Bonds	Index	1,020.6	Income	1.0%	More on Bonds
	YTD change	2.1%	Capital growth	1.1%	
Shares	Index	1,052.7	Income	0.4%	More on Shares
	YTD change	+5.3%	Capital growth	4.9%	
Property	Index	1,030.4	Income	0.6%	More on Property
	YTD change	+3.0%	Capital growth	2.4%	
Analysis: Insight Financial Consulting					

INSIGHT INVESTING: COMPARING THE BIG FOUR

Of course, selecting wealth-creating assets is not all about risk and reward. Liquidity, term, and capital are also relevant. The following table compares the key features of all four wealth-creating assets.

	Savings accounts	Bonds	Shares	Property
Return	Low	Medium	High	Very high
Liquidity	✔	✔	✔	✗
Risk	✔	✔	✗	✗
Term	✔	✗	✗	✗
Capital	✔	✗	✗	✗

✔ denotes that the issue is not usually significant
✗ denotes that the issue is always significant

THE BIG FOUR: KEY FEATURES COMPARED

Savings accounts tend to be highly liquid, low risk, can provide short-term returns, and require little capital investment. At the other end of the scale, property is the highest-risk investment and is also highly illiquid, offers returns that may take a long time to achieve, and requires a significant capital investment. In deciding which wealth-creating assets are right for you, you need to decide what sacrifices you are prepared to make to achieve the higher rates of return on offer.

One factor that can have a significant impact when it comes to selecting appropriate wealth-creating assets is where you are in your lifecycle.

EARLY CAREER	MID/LATE CAREER	RETIREMENT
	⬆️⬇️ 🏠	
Savings accounts	Shares and/or property	Bonds
Priority is to protect funds against inflation	Priority is to grow wealth	Priority is to generate income

THE IMPACT OF LIFECYCLE ON INVESTMENT SELECTION

As you start out on your career funds are scarce, so whatever money you do have you will want to protect against inflation. Not surprisingly at this stage, savings accounts tend to be the most favored investment vehicle.

As you progress through your working life and income increases, this is the time you will want to focus on building up your wealth to enhance your standard of living and provide a fund for retirement. The two main investment opportunities that satisfy this need are shares and property. It is during this phase that many people turn to a third party such as a financial adviser and/or a fund manager to make their investment decisions for them. As I stress throughout this book, making your own decisions could save you a small fortune in fees and thereby improve returns substantially.

As retirement approaches, you should have built up a fund that enables you to enjoy a regular income. At this stage, bonds tend to be the most appropriate wealth-creating asset, as they can offer fixed rates of return over many years that (if chosen carefully) have minimal risk.

These are the most favored types of investments as individuals progress through their lifecycle, though this does not mean that they are the only types of investment used at each stage. During mid and late career, although considerable sums are often invested in shares and property, savings accounts and bonds may also be utilized. In retirement it is common for individuals to maintain a share portfolio. Indeed, it is quite possible to have all four types of wealth-creating asset through most of the lifecycle. What we are highlighting here is where the emphasis tends to be placed.

THE ESSENTIALS

* **Remember the tradeoffs** – every investment opportunity involves trading off return against liquidity, risk, term, and capital.
* **Consider savings accounts** – their primary use is to protect funds against inflation.
* **Consider bonds** – their primary use is to generate a regular income.
* **Consider shares and property** – these provide the most significant opportunity to grow wealth.
* **Be aware of the lifecycle** – where you are in your lifecycle will influence which wealth-creating assets are most appropriate to your needs.

4

THE 6R APPROACH TO INVESTING

Here are a few alarming facts relating to private investors: many lose money because they invest in a hot tip provided by a friend or colleague; many lose money because they do not understand what they are investing in; many lose money because they do not appreciate the risks; many lose money because they invest and then forget about it; many lose money because they had to sell their investments unexpectedly; many lose money because they do not know how to spot a good investment.

All of the above issues can be attributed to lack of discipline. Investing is all about finding a good investment and then managing it. If you make good decisions, you will make money; if you make bad decisions, you will lose money. The trouble is that too many people allow emotions to enter the fray – and your worst enemy when making investment decisions is getting emotional. Just because you like an opportunity does not mean it is a good investment, just as not liking an opportunity does not make it a bad investment.

The 6Rs of investing

Discipline needs to be incorporated within the investment decision-making process. We know that at the very heart of investing is a tradeoff between risk and reward and, given that both risk and reward begin with the letter R, a marketing manager might be tempted to promote them as the "2Rs of investing," the two concepts on which every investor should focus their attention. While it is true that the higher the rate of return you achieve on your funds the better your investment is doing, it is not necessarily true that in order to achieve a higher rate of return you need to take on more risk, however. As we have seen, there are other issues that need to be considered: liquidity, the term of the investment, and the amount of capital that needs to be invested. Even after you have parted with your money, there is no guarantee that the investment is going to perform as expected, so you need to remain vigilant.

A key message I always endeavor to get across when I am teaching people how to make investment decisions is that a prerequisite to making a good decision is to ensure that consideration has been paid to all the relevant issues. I would argue that in fact there are 6Rs of investing, not two. Only by being aware of what these 6Rs are can you ever hope to make investment decisions that really will grow your money and thereby enhance your future lifestyle.

First of all, you need to be able to recognize an investment opportunity when it arises. If you cannot spot an opportunity, how can you ever hope to exploit it? That is the first R – RECOGNIZE. Having recognized an opportunity, you need to identify the potential rate of return; you need to be aware of how you can win. This provides the second R – REWARD. The problem is that there is a tradeoff between risk and reward so, having examined the reward, the next logical step is to look at the risk; you need to be aware of how you can lose. This is the third R – RISK. But risk is not the only issue that can affect the performance of an investment: you also need to research how liquidity, term, and capital can influence the performance of your

investment. This is the fourth R – RESEARCH. It is only
when you get to this stage that you can make an informed
decision. You need to review what you have learned about
this opportunity and decide whether it is right for you. This
is the fifth R – REVIEW. But even when you have made your
decision and parted with your cash, it is essential that you
remain vigilant. Circumstances can change and you need
to be prepared to take action if your wealth-creating assets
are not performing as expected: you need to revisit your
investments on a regular basis. This is the sixth R – REVISIT.

THE 6R APPROACH TO INVESTING
Recognize
Reward
Risk
Research
Review
Revisit

These six elements should be incorporated in every investment decision. You will no doubt have noticed that
each element logically leads on to the next, so what we
have identified here is a process that breaks investment
decision-making down into six stages, with each stage
incorporating one of the six Rs. Let's look at this process in
a little more depth, step by step; it will also be used as the
template for the more detailed chapters to follow.

Stage 1: Recognize

At the outset you need to recognize and be aware of
the investment opportunities available and identify those
that are most suitable for you.

Stage 2 - Reward

Just because you spot an opportunity, that does not necessarily mean that you should take advantage of it. It is one thing to say an opportunity exists to grow your money; it is a very different thing to decide if it is worth pursuing. You need to identify the potential rate of return, but there is more to the reward stage than you might think. History has taught us time and again that looking at past performance is not a good indicator of what to expect in the future, so the first challenge is being able to identify anticipated future rates of return.

There are three forces in operation that can significantly limit the rate of return you achieve:

* Inflation
* Tax
* Fees

Increasing prices erode the value of your future returns. Although you cannot control inflation, you need to be aware of how it can affect the performance of your investments, as failure to do so can result in you ending up worse off than when you started. Secondly, there is tax – you need to know the impact that tax will have on your rate of return. Being alert to any tax-efficient and tax-free investment vehicles can improve rates of return significantly. Finally, if you decide to use the services of third parties to make your investment decisions for you (such as financial advisers and fund managers), you will have to pay fees. These are often not transparent to the investor and can run into tens of thousands of dollars over a typical individual's lifetime. Simply being aware of fees and how to minimize them can have a dramatic impact on the performance of your investments and on your future lifestyle.

Stage 3 – Risk

The third stage involves identifying what the risks are and, most importantly, identifying any actions that can be taken to mitigate them. Knowing how to manage risk is a key skill for any aspiring independent investor.

Stage 4 – Research

In the next stage you need to research the other three factors, in addition to risk, that can have an impact on the suitability of an investment: liquidity, risk, and term. As far as liquidity is concerned, it is pointless investing money if you cannot access it when needed, so you have to confirm how readily you can gain access to your cash. You also need to ascertain if there any penalty charges or fees you will incur when doing this. It is not uncommon for people to invest money with fund managers and then unexpectedly require access to their cash, thereby triggering onerous exit charges, with the result that they receive back significantly less than they paid in.

When it comes to term, depending on the investment, you may have to be prepared to tie up your money for a considerable period of time before you achieve any form of return.

Finally, the amount you have to invest (the capital) needs to be considered. If you have $5,000 available, savings accounts and shares would be reasonable options, but property would not.

Stage 5 – Review

Having completed the first four stages of the 6R approach, it is time to make the decision, and this is where the fifth R comes into play – review. Before you part with your money, you need to review what you have found out:

* What is the rate of return?
* How will inflation, tax, and fees affect this?
* What are the risks and what actions can be taken to minimize them?
* Do you regard the possibility of losing some or all of your investment as low, medium, or high?
* How accessible is your money?
* How long do you expect this investment to last?
* How much do you need to invest?

Only by answering all of these questions can you decide whether a potential investment is right for you. It is at this stage that you must make the decision whether or not to part with your cash.

Stage 6 – Revisit

Complacency is one of the greatest enemies of the investor. Many people forget about their investments once they've committed the funds, but the world is constantly changing and so too are investment opportunities, so vigilance is key. For the sixth R – revisit – you must have the discipline to revisit your investments regularly, reevaluate their current and potential performance, and always be prepared to reallocate your funds if better rates of return are available elsewhere. As I often say to delegates on my training programs, "You should date investments, not marry them!"

GROW YOUR OWN MONEY
Always adopt the 6R approach when making any investment decision.

The complete decision-making process

This six-stage approach to making any investment decision is not some get-rich-quick scheme that promises to make you millions, but a way of introducing discipline into the decision-making process, a discipline that forces you to step back and be objective.

If you want to make a well-informed investment decision, you have no choice but to address the 6Rs in some manner. Many erroneous investment decisions can be traced back to individuals omitting to address one or more of the 6Rs. Ensure you don't make the same mistake.

The process can be summarized as below:

* Stage 1 – RECOGNIZE the opportunity.
* Stage 2 – Identify the potential REWARD.
* Stage 3 – Assess the RISK.
* Stage 4 – RESEARCH other factors affecting performance.
* Stage 5 – REVIEW the findings of Stages 1 to 4.
* Stage 6 – REVISIT your investments regularly.

THE ESSENTIALS

* **Remember the 6Rs of investing** – every investment decision should include recognize, reward, risk, research, review, and revisit.

* **Always apply the 6R approach** – it provides a structured method for assessing any investment opportunity.

* **Avoid making poor decisions** – many erroneous investment decisions result from omitting one or more of the 6Rs.

5

SPARE CASH IS DEAD CASH:

INVESTING IN SAVINGS ACCOUNTS

When most people are considering what to do with their spare cash, the first type of investment that springs to mind is a savings account. It is a commonly held view that investing in savings accounts is straightforward: you deposit money and you earn interest – you can't lose. Unfortunately, this form of investment is not quite as straightforward as might at first appear. Many people invest in savings accounts and think they're enhancing their wealth, whereas in reality they end up worse off than when they started.

In this chapter we're going to examine savings accounts in some depth and look at how you can determine whether or not they offer an appropriate haven for your hard-earned cash. We're going to achieve this by applying the 6R approach to this specific investment opportunity.

Stage 1 – Recognize

The first stage of the 6R approach is being able to recognize the opportunity. When it comes to savings, many people assume all that is involved is seeking out the type of account that best suits their needs and then identifying the most favorable interest rate available. This can prove to be a real challenge, as there are often a wide range of interest rates to choose from. In order to ensure that you secure the most favorable rate, it's worth dedicating some time to understanding why interest rates on savings accounts can differ in the first place.

Financial institutions want your money so that they can loan it out and pursue their own investment strategies. Not surprisingly, they will want to raise the funds they need as cost efficiently as possible – the less they need to pay out for the use of your money, the more profit they can make. It follows that financial institutions need some method for enticing savers to act in a cost-effective manner.

The first point to note is that what concerns banks is the total cost of funds: the total amount they have to pay to access your money. The second point is that the total cost of funds comprises two core elements: interest and transaction costs (the costs of executing receipts and withdrawals). If they can encourage you to reduce transaction costs, they can afford to reward you with more interest.

There are three ways they can achieve this. They can encourage you to indulge in long-term deposits – a financial institution would prefer you to deposit $1,000 for a year, rather than make 12 consecutive $1,000 deposits for one month each. They like large deposits – a financial institution would prefer you to make one deposit of $1,000, rather than ten deposits of $100 each. Finally, they would like you to conduct transactions in a cost-efficient manner. If you're prepared to perform transactions over the internet, by telephone, or by post, this is far more cost effective than conducting transactions face to face in a branch. We can conclude that an ideal transaction, from a financial institution's point of view, would be a $1 million deposit for five years conducted over the internet. The closer you can get to this ideal, the higher the rate of interest you should be able to achieve.

Invest for a   **Invest a**   **Be**
LONG PERIOD   **LARGE SUM**   **COST EFFICIENT**

THREE WAYS TO ACHIEVE HIGHER INTEREST RATES

For most financial institutions, the most potent of these attributes is the period of time. The longer they know they can rely on having the use of your funds, the higher the interest rate they tend to offer. The lowest rates are likely to be offered on instant access accounts, where you can get hold of your funds immediately without incurring any penalty charges. Higher rates are usually offered on accounts where, in order to avoid penalty charges, you have to give advance notice of intended withdrawals, typically 30, 60, or 90 days. The highest rates tend to be reserved for fixed-term deposits, where money is invested for a fixed period such as one, two, or three years. So when looking for a savings account, you need to decide at the outset how much you are prepared to invest, for how long, and what method of transacting business best suits you.

Stage 2 – Reward

Having identified a savings account that may appeal, the second stage is to identify the potential reward, which means ascertaining the rate of interest you will earn. Regrettably, this is nowhere near as straightforward as you might think, because there are three different rates of interest that apply to every account:

∗   The gross rate.
∗   The post-tax rate.
∗   The real rate.

Failing to understand what these various rates mean and, more importantly, how they affect the performance of your savings can often result in you losing money, and you may not even realize it's happening. What we are about to cover might seem a bit involved at the outset, but if you want to grow your money in a savings account, you really do need to understand this.

The **gross rate of interest** is the rate of interest you tend to see quoted on advertisements and in information leaflets. If an account says that it pays 5% per annum, this means that it will pay $5 interest each year on every $100 invested. Now for some bad news: this is not the interest you will necessarily receive.

In many countries tax has to be paid on any interest you earn. This may be deducted from your interest before it is paid into your account, or you may be required to pay the tax later on. Either way, the overall effect is the same: the interest you earn is not what you receive. Suppose that you invest $100, the quoted rate of interest is 5%, and the tax rate on savings income is 30%. In this instance, out of the $5 interest you are due, 30% of it ($1.50) will be payable to the government, leaving you with $3.50. Consequently, the value of your savings will only grow by $3.50 each year on every $100 invested, so the rate of interest you will achieve will be 3.5% (not 5%). This is your **post-tax rate of interest**. You might be tempted to think that at least your wealth is going up, even if only by a small amount, but ironically your wealth may be going down. How can this possibly be the case?

Inflation erodes the purchasing power of money: over time prices of goods and services tend to go up. If inflation is 4% per annum, this means that prices in one year's time will be 4% higher than they are now. In other words, if something costs $100 today, its cost will increase to $104 over the next 12 months. The **real rate of interest** is the difference between your post-tax rate of return and the rate of inflation.

KEY MEASURE

Real rate of interest	=	Gross rate of interest
		– Tax payable
		– Rate of inflation

Suppose that a savings account offers 5% interest per annum, you pay tax at 30%, and inflation is 4.5%. Your real rate of interest can be worked out as follows:

Real rate of interest
= Gross rate of interest of 5%
   LESS tax payable of 1.5% (i.e., 30% of the gross rate of 5%)
   LESS rate of inflation of 4.5%
= Real rate of interest of –1%

Let's follow this through step by step. Suppose that you invest $100 in this account. The gross rate says that you will earn $5 interest during the year (5% of your $100 investment). The tax rate says that 30% of this interest is payable to the government and that works out at $1.50, so tax is reducing your rate of interest by 1.5%. This leaves you with a post-tax interest rate of 3.5%, which means that you will end up with $103.50 in a year's time.

We still need to address the inflation issue, however. An inflation rate of 4.5% tells us that something costing

$100 today will cost $104.50 in a year's time. The problem is that depositing the same amount of money in the savings account will only give you $103.50, which means that in a year's time you will not be able to afford what you can today – not a desirable result! This is where the final part of the calculation comes into play. You need to deduct the rate of inflation from your post-tax interest rate. By deducting an inflation rate of 4.5% from the post-tax rate of interest of 3.5%, we arrive at the answer of minus 1%, which says that you will be approximately 1% worse off in a year's time; you will be able to afford 1% fewer goods and services.

I should emphasize that this is an approximate figure. I know that some pedants will argue that if something costs $104.50 in a year's time and you only end up with $103.50, you are in fact 0.96% worse off, but as far as I am concerned the difference in results is negligible. In the spirit of keeping things simple, all you need to know is roughly how much better off or worse off you are going to be after allowing for inflation. Incidentally, there is a formula that allows you to work out the exact real rate of interest, but trust me, you really do not want to see it!

GROW YOUR OWN MONEY
Always check the real rate of interest before investing in a savings account.

Given that a prime objective for many savers is to protect their money from the ravages of inflation, it makes sense to check the real rate of interest being achieved on your savings on a regular basis. A positive real rate of interest means that your spending power will increase over time.

while a negative real rate of interest means that your spending power will diminish. Establishing the real rate of interest is one of the few calculations in this book where the onus is on you to work it out; sadly, financial institutions will not do the calculation for you.

An alternative way to determine whether or not interest rates on savings accounts are beating inflation is to work out the minimum gross rate of interest you need to earn to ensure that you are no worse off. Provided that the advertised rate is above this figure, you know that your purchasing power will increase. Fortunately, there is a calculation that enables us to identify this figure and the good news is that you only need two numbers to work it out: the rate of inflation and the rate at which you are liable to pay tax on your savings income.

KEY MEASURE

Minimum acceptable gross savings rate

$$= \frac{\text{Rate of inflation}}{\text{100\% − Tax rate}} \times 100\%$$

If we stick with the figures from the previous example – inflation is 4.5% and you pay 30% tax on your income – the minimum acceptable gross savings rate needed to ensure that your wealth is not decreasing can be calculated as follows:

Minimum acceptable gross savings rate

$$= \frac{\text{Rate of inflation of 4.5\%}}{\text{100\% − 30\% Tax rate}} \times 100\%$$

$$= \frac{4.5}{70} \times 100\%$$

$$= 6.4\%$$

As with the previous calculation, this is one you have to work out for yourself. Understandably, financial institutions are not keen to highlight savings accounts that can't keep up with increasing prices.

Let's make sure that we understand the logic. The first step involves taking the rate of inflation, which is 4.5%. We must then divide this by 100% less the tax rate of 30%, which works out at 70%. Dividing 4.5 by 70 and then multiplying the answer by 100 gives the minimum acceptable rate of 6.4%. This is the gross interest rate that needs to be advertised for your wealth to remain unaltered.

You now know that if a savings account offers in excess of 6.4%, your purchasing power is going to increase, while anything below this rate will reduce your purchasing power. Suppose you are looking at six potential savings accounts offering gross rates of 3.8%, 6.9%, 5.8%, 7.2%, 4.5%, and 6.2%. If inflation is 4.5% and you pay tax at 30%, only two of these accounts offer the opportunity to beat inflation, because only two of them offer gross rates in excess of 6.4%.

GROW YOUR OWN MONEY
Knowing the minimum acceptable gross savings rate enables you readily to identify savings accounts that really will grow your money.

Insight Investing provides details of the minimum accept-able gross savings rates that need to be paid on UK sav-ings accounts in order to keep up with inflation. Provided that you know the local rate of inflation and the tax rates payable, a similar table can be easily constructed for any country.

Minimum Interest Rates Required to keep up with Inflation

As at 24th March 2014

TAX STATUS	MINIMUM GROSS INTEREST RATE REQUIRED TO KEEP UP WITH INFLATION (RPI) %
▶ If you are a non-payer or the account is tax-free (e.g. ISA)	2.8
▶ If you are a basic rate taxpayer paying 20% income tax	3.5
▶ If you are a higher rate taxpayer paying 40% income tax	4.7
▶ If you are an additional rate taxpayer paying 45% income tax	5.1

Analysis: Insight Financial Consulting

INSIGHT INVESTING: MINIMUM ACCEPTABLE
GROSS SAVINGS RATES

One way you might be able to improve the real rate of interest you achieve is to locate and invest in a tax-free savings account, if there are any available. But a word of warning: just because an account is tax free doesn't nec-essarily mean that it will provide a good rate of return. Sometimes taxable savings accounts will produce a better rate of return even after paying tax. To decide whether or not a tax-free investment is worthwhile, you need to com-pare its advertised rate against the post-tax rates of interest that you could earn on alternative taxable accounts.

There is one other method available to improve the rate of return that is very low risk, and that is to use your savings to pay off any debts you may have. Bizarre as it might seem, many people have savings while also being in debt, yet the interest rates charged on loans are usually significantly higher than the interest rates earned on savings.

Suppose you have a bank loan charging an annual interest rate of 10% and a savings account paying a gross annual interest rate of 5%. The first issue that needs to be addressed is tax, as this reduces the rate of return on savings. We noted in a previous example that if you pay tax at 30% on a savings account paying a gross annual rate of 5%, your post-tax rate of interest will be 3.5%. Now you have a choice: you can put $100 in a savings account on which you will receive interest after tax of $3.50 each year, or you can use the same $100 to pay off part of your loan and save yourself $10 loan interest a year. Adopting the latter option would mean that, on every $100 of savings you use to pay off your loan, you will be $6.50 better off each year (netting off the $10 saving in loan interest against the $3.50 savings interest being forgone). Congratulations, you have just increased a post-tax rate of interest of 3.5% by 6.5 percentage points up to 10%; not bad for doing very little.

Before pursuing this course of action, do check that you will not suffer penalty charges for either withdrawing your savings or repaying the loan early. If penalties are applicable, you may have to do some extra research to make sure that the additional charges don't wipe out the benefit of the loan interest you will be saving.

This principle of using savings to pay off loans can apply even when the savings rate exceeds the loan rate. In this situation you may be tempted to think that you should always keep your money in a savings account, as the interest you are earning is more than the interest you are paying out.

Suppose you have a savings account that pays 10% gross per annum, you have a loan that costs you 8% per annum, and you pay 40% tax on your savings income. In this scenario, on every $100 you have in the savings account, you are earning $10 interest, out of which $4 is payable in tax, leaving you with $6. At the same time, on every $100 you are borrowing, you are paying out $8 interest. If you withdrew $100 from your savings account, you would lose $6 worth of income, but if you then used that $100 to pay off part of the loan, you would save yourself $8 loan interest – you would end up being $2 better off. In the world of savings accounts nothing is as obvious as it seems.

Stage 3 – Risk

We can now move on to the third stage of the 6R approach: assess the risk. To the uninitiated, to say that savings accounts are risky might come as a bit of a surprise, but in reality there are two types of risk associated with this form of investment:

* Inflation.
* Institutional risk.

Inflation has already been addressed. This risk can be overcome by ensuring that you are earning a positive real rate of interest.

Institutional risk refers to the possibility that the financial institution to which you entrust your money could fail. There are two ways in which you can tackle this problem. First, choose who you place your money with carefully. Secondly, you can spread your risk by holding your savings across several institutions so that if one of them should go under, you will not have lost all of your money.

Stage 4 – Research

Now we are in a position to move on to the fourth stage – research other factors affecting performance. In addition to risk, three other factors ought to be addressed in order to assess the suitability of an investment: liquidity, term, and capital. This involves studying the terms and conditions that relate to the account under review.

When it comes to liquidity, many savings accounts offer instant access to cash, but intrinsically linked to liquidity is term. We noted earlier in the chapter that you may be able to achieve a higher rate of interest by investing in a savings account where you have to give notice (which may be months) of any proposed withdrawals, or agree to deposit your money for a fixed period of time (which may run into years). Finally, the capital requirement will be determined by the minimum deposit required, which can sometimes be as little as $1.

Stage 5 – Review

You have now completed the first four stages and are devastatingly close to making your investment decision – but don't allow your enthusiasm to run away with you. Are you going to invest in this savings account or not? This is the fifth stage of the 6R approach – review the findings in Stages 1 to 4:

* Does the account deliver a positive real rate of interest?

✳   Does the financial institution seem like a safe place
    to put your money?
✳   Are you comfortable with the account features in
    terms of access to cash, the term of the investment,
    and the amount you need to invest?

If you have no concerns on these various issues, you can
part with your money. However, if you are uncomfort-
able with any of your findings, either discard the opportunity altogether or at least do some more investigating.
Remember, you don't have to invest if you don't want to.

Stage 6 – Revisit

And so to the sixth and final stage – revisit your investments regularly. You've done all the hard work: you've
found a savings account that exactly matches your needs
and you've deposited your cash. Now what many people
do is just sit back and wait for the interest to roll in. In fact,
this is the worst thing you can possibly do.

One of the most common reasons for savers receiv-
ing paltry rates of interest is **savings inertia**. They secure
an account that appears competitive at the time and then,
having deposited their money, they simply leave it there.
Interest rates can change and a good rate today can easily become an appalling rate tomorrow. To maximize your
returns, you must be prepared to move your funds if more
profitable opportunities arise elsewhere.

Don't be complacent: revisit your savings accounts on
a regular basis and check how they are doing. A few minutes a month checking the interest rates on offer can prove
to be a very profitable activity.

THE ESSENTIALS

* **RECOGNIZE** – find an account that appeals to your needs. Remember, financial institutions like long-term, high-value, cost-efficient transactions.
* **REWARD** – tax and inflation eat away at your returns. Calculate the real rate of interest or, alternatively, the minimum acceptable gross rate of interest needed to beat inflation.
* **RISK** – think inflation and institution. Ensure that you are achieving a positive real rate of return. If you have a large sum to invest, be prepared to spread it over several institutions.
* **RESEARCH** – check liquidity, term, and capital. Ensure that the access to cash, the term of the investment, and the amount to be invested match your requirements.
* **REVIEW** – looking back at what you have learned about this opportunity, is this the right savings account for you?
* **REVISIT** – remain vigilant. A good rate of interest today does not guarantee a good rate tomorrow.

6

RAISING THE STAKES:

INVESTING IN BONDS

You would like to achieve better returns than are available on savings accounts, but you want an investment that is less risky than shares. Welcome to the world of government and corporate bonds. In this chapter we are going to examine how the 6R approach to investing can be applied to the bond market.

Stage 1 – Recognize

Traditionally the bond market has very much been the preserve of large institutional investors (such as pension funds and banks), with minimum transaction values typically being $100,000 or more. Fortunately this market is gradually becoming more accessible to the average person as those minimum transaction values fall.

Before considering investing in bonds, you need to understand how they work. A good starting point is to review some of the jargon that is associated with this specific type of investment. Just as a word of warning, the bond market loves jargon – the philosophy in this market is very much: Why keep things simple if you can make them sound complicated? Don't let that put you off, though. Once you understand the terminology, the principles underpinning this market are pretty straightforward.

The first term that we need to address is the **issuer**, which is the organization that is raising funds through the issue of bonds. There are four main types:

* Governments.
* Supranational entities (international organizations backed by a number of governments, such as the European Investment Bank).
* Government agencies and local government authorities.
* Companies.

Governments form a very significant class of player in the bond market. Government expenditure can only be financed in one of two ways: through taxes or via borrowing. Governments rely on borrowing to finance a significant amount of their expenditure on transport, healthcare, education, defense, and so forth. Bonds issued by some governments, such as those from the US and the UK, are often regarded as of the highest credit quality (almost risk free). As such, rates of return on these bonds tend to be very low and are often used as benchmarks against which to assess the performance of other bond issuers. Bonds are also issued by supranational entities, which are typically also regarded as being of very high credit quality. Government agencies and local government authorities can also issue bonds but, because they do not tend to be backed by central government, they are often perceived as slightly lower credit quality than their government counterparts. Finally, regular trading companies (which includes financial institutions) also need to borrow to help finance their operations. Depending on the company involved, the credit quality can range from very good to very poor.

The next piece of jargon that needs to be addressed is the **nominal value**. Also known as the principal or par value, this is the amount that will be paid back to the bond-holder when the bond is redeemed. If a bond has a nominal value of $1,000, this tells you that the issuer will pay back $1,000 at the end of the loan term. It is worth noting that, just like bank notes, bonds can be issued in a variety of denominations, such as $1,000, $10,000, or $50,000. This brings us neatly on to another term: the **redemption date**, which is the date on which the issuer agrees to pay back the nominal amount.

The final piece of jargon you need to understand at this stage relates to the rate of interest payable. As you can imagine in this market, the view is very much: Why use the term interest rate (which everyone would understand) when you can call it the **coupon** (which very few people will understand)? Also known as the coupon rate, this is the annual interest that will be paid, expressed as a percentage of the nominal value. There is some logic behind it being called the coupon. Historically, when bonds were issued in paper format (it is mostly electronic these days), they had coupons attached that the bondholder would detach to claim the appropriate interest payment, hence the term coupon.

We are now well placed to make sense of a bond issue. Suppose a company needs to raise money and issues a bond with a 6% coupon and a redemption date of October 31, 2025. This means that the company will pay $6 interest each year on every $100 of nominal value held by the bondholder, with full repayment of the nominal amount taking place on October 31, 2025. One of the big attractions of bonds is the fact that investors know in advance the amount of interest they are going to earn each year and the exact day they are going to get their money back. Not surprisingly, then, the majority of investors tend to turn to the bond market when they want to generate a long-term regular income stream.

Like all investors, you will of course want to achieve the highest possible rate of return. In this market there are two overriding factors that drive this: risk and term. The higher the risk attached to a bond issue, the higher the rate of return tends to be in order to entice you to part with your money. At the same time, rates of return also tend to increase the longer the bond has to run until redemption.

When it comes to identifying bonds that may be of interest at the outset, you need to decide for how long you are prepared to invest your money. There are many websites and publications that detail bonds currently available to the independent investor. What you will be looking for are bonds that have redemption dates that closely match your intended investment horizon. (The risk issue will be addressed later in the decision-making process.)

Stage 2 – Reward

The rate of return achievable on bonds – the reward – is determined by two factors: the price you pay and the coupon. Let's look at some typical details that you may see reported for an individual bond.

Issuer	Coupon	Redemption date	Price	Flat yield	Redemption yield	Period of coupon
Gottmore Khash	5.00	31 Dec 25	96.50	5.18	5.50	12 months

TYPICAL REPORTED DETAILS FOR A BOND ISSUE

This may look like a lot to take in, but it is quite straight-forward when you get to grips with it. The convention is to describe bonds in the following order: issuer, coupon, and maturity date. In this instance the bond would be described as "Gottmore Khash 5% December 31, 2025." Addressing each of the reported items in turn, in this instance you can see that the name of the issuer is Gottmore Khash. The coupon, as you know, is the annual interest that will be paid expressed as a percentage of the nominal value. Here for every $100 of nominal you own, you will receive $5 interest each year. Next is the redemption date, and in this instance the issuer agrees to pay back the nominal value on December 31, 2025.

It is important to appreciate that if a bond has a nominal value of $1,000, that is the amount you are going to receive back on the redemption date regardless of how much you pay for the bond in the first place. Bear in mind that bonds are tradable and as a result the price is not fixed. This may work in your favor – you may end up selling or redeeming a bond for more than you paid for it – but it can also work against you, with you selling or redeeming the bond for less than you paid for it. So what determines bond prices? To understand this you need to know how bond prices affect rate of return.

You will note that in the case of Gottmore Khash the bond price is 96.50. What does this tell us? It is convention to quote bond prices as a percentage of the nominal value. So a bond price of 96.50 says that the bond price is currently 96.5% of the nominal value. If the bond has a nominal value of $1,000, the current price is $965; if the bond has a nominal value of $10,000, the current price is $9,650, and so on.

There are three potential pricing scenarios when you buy a bond:

* The price is less than 100.
* The price is exactly 100.
* The price is more than 100.

When the price is less than 100 you are paying less than the nominal value, so on the redemption date you will receive back more than you paid for the bond. This will clearly have a favorable impact on your rate of return. When the price is exactly 100, the price is said to be at par, in which case for every $100 you pay for a bond you will get the same amount back on the redemption date. Finally, if the price is more than 100, you will receive back less than you paid for the bond, which will clearly have an adverse impact on your rate of return.

Now you may be thinking that all you have to do is make sure that you buy bonds for less than 100, because that way you will be improving your rate of return. Yet investors are often prepared to buy bonds when the price is above 100. To appreciate why they are willing to do this, we need to turn our attention specifically to the rate of return.

The rate of return on bonds is known as the yield and two types are commonly quoted. The most straightforward is **flat yield**, which expresses the annual coupon payable as a percentage of the current bond price.

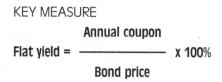

KEY MEASURE

$$\text{Flat yield} = \frac{\text{Annual coupon}}{\text{Bond price}} \times 100\%$$

Suppose that a bond is paying a 5.7% coupon and the price is 95. That means that $5.70 interest is payable on every $100 of nominal value, for which you will only be paying $95. In this circumstance the flat yield would be worked out as follows:

$$\text{Flat yield} = \frac{\text{Annual coupon of \$5.70}}{\text{Bond price of \$95.00}} \times 100\%$$

$$= 6\%$$

Each year you will be receiving 6% of your initial investment back in the form of interest. This is clearly useful when assessing the income potential of a bond, but it does have a serious limitation. It ignores the fact that, if you buy a bond at a price that differs from its nominal value, there is also a capital gain (or loss) that will crystallize when the bond is redeemed.

Suppose that redemption of this particular bond is scheduled in one year's time and, to keep things simple, let's assume it has a nominal value of $100. The flat yield is ignoring the fact that you are also going to gain by buying the bond for $95 now in the knowledge that you are going to get back $100 in a year's time, providing you with an extra $5 profit on the deal. Redemption yield looks at the annual coupon payable and the annual capital gain (or loss) combined as a percentage of the current bond price.

KEY MEASURE

$$\text{Redemption yield} = \frac{\text{Annual coupon + Annual capital gain}}{\text{Bond price}} \times 100\%$$

The redemption yield for the current bond under review works out as follows:

Redemption yield

$$= \frac{\text{Annual coupon of \$5.70} + \text{Annual capital gain of \$5}}{\text{Bond price of \$95}} \times 100\%$$

$$= 11.3\%$$

So allowing for the capital gain you will enjoy if you hold the bond to maturity, you will achieve an annual rate of return of 11.3%.

GROW YOUR OWN MONEY
Before investing in bonds, always check the redemption yield.

Returning to Gottmore Khash, the two yield figures should now make sense. The flat yield of 5.18% tells you that the annual interest to be paid will be 5.18% of the purchase price, while the redemption yield says that if you hold the bond to maturity, your overall annual return (including the capital gain) works out at 5.50%.

The only item left is the period of the coupon, which states how frequently interest is paid. Typically it will be either every six months or annually; in the case of Gottmore Khash, interest will be paid annually.

Redemption yields for individual bond issues can be found on a variety of investor websites. Insight Investing provides a summary of the average redemption yields available on UK government and corporate bonds.

So now you can make sense of bond data – well, almost. There is one final twist in the tale. The price

Government and Corporate Bond Performance

As at 24th March 2014

TERM TO REDEMPTION	AVERAGE ANNUAL YIELD IF HELD TO REDEMPTION	
	UK GOVERNMENT %	COMPANIES %
▶ 1 year	0.4	0.7
▶ 2 years	0.7	1.3
▶ 3 years	1.1	2.2
▶ 4 years	1.7	2.3
▶ 5 years	2.0	3.5
▶ 10 years	2.7	4.4
▶ 15 years	3.3	4.4
▶ 20 years	3.4	4.5
▶ 30 years	3.5	5.1

Data sources: London Stock Exchange, Thomson Reuters

Analysis: Insight Financial Consulting

INSIGHT INVESTING: REDEMPTION YIELDS

reported when you are looking at the trading details of a bond is known as the **clean price**. In the case of Gottmore Khash we know that for every $100 of nominal bought, the buyer will need to pay $96.50. This assumes that you buy the bond either on the date of issue or (if the bond has already been issued) immediately after the latest coupon has been paid. This is rarely the case, though.

Suppose that you want to buy bonds issued by Gottmore Khash, but it is June 30. On December 31 you know that you will receive a $5 coupon for every $100 of nominal you hold. The seller is entitled to half of this sum for the first six months of the year. **Accrued interest** is the additional sum that needs to be paid, in addition to the clean price, to compensate the seller for the interest they

should have received. In this instance, $2.50 accrued inter-
est will need to be paid to the seller.

Time for a bit more jargon. The **dirty price** is the
clean price plus any accrued interest, which is the effective price you pay, and in this instance it works out to be
$99 per $100 of nominal. Now, you would not be alone if
you thought that somehow you were being conned at this
stage, as the clean price is clearly $96.50 per $100 of nominal, yet you are going to end up paying the dirty price
of $99. However, think about what will happen if you
buy $100 worth of nominal. You will pay $99 now, but
at the end of the year you will receive a full year's interest of $5, even though you have only owned the bond
for six months. So although you will be paying an extra
$2.50 now, you will in effect be refunded that money in
six months' time.

One final point needs to be made regarding rates of
return. For savings accounts, the focus is on real rates of
return; that is, after allowing for the impact of tax and
inflation. For bonds and other forms of wealth-creating
asset, the focus is far more on pre-tax rates of return.
This is not because tax and inflation are not relevant – of
course they are, and inflation will be addressed in the next
section – but the objectives are different. The main use of
savings accounts is to protect money against the effects
of inflation, which explains why knowing the real rate of
return is so important. Bonds, shares, and property are
perceived as providing opportunities to grow the value of
money in real terms. What is needed in this instance is a
fast and effective means of comparing alternative investment opportunities, and the pre-tax rate of return provides a way of doing this.

Stage 3 – Risk

There are five main risks of which you need to be aware when looking at bonds:

* Market risk.
* Issue-specific risk.
* Inflation.
* Interest rate risk.
* Default risk.

The fact that there are five different risks to be aware of does not mean that bonds are high risk, however. In many instances bonds are regarded as very low risk and, as we shall discover, most of the risks can be readily overcome.

Market risk refers to the fact that bond prices can change from day to day depending on supply and demand. Although the variations are often quite minor, you ought to be aware that they can happen.

Issue-specific risk refers to the fact that some bond issues have characteristics that may be detrimental to the bond holders. For example, some bonds have a call option, whereby the issuer may reserve the right to redeem the bond early, which may not work in the investors' favor. Countering this risk involves checking the terms and conditions of the bond issue to make sure that there are no clauses that could adversely affect your returns. Fortunately, most issues are pretty straightforward, with a fixed coupon and a fixed redemption date.

The next risk is inflation, which is a significant risk when investing in any form of fixed-interest security. You need to be convinced that the redemption yield on offer will keep ahead of inflation; the longer the term to maturity, the more significant this risk becomes.

Although the risks mentioned so far are relevant, the two that preoccupy most bond investors are interest rate risk and default risk. Interest rate risk is relevant if you anticipate having to sell bonds prior to their redemption date. In this circumstance you should note that bond prices are inversely related to interest rate changes: when interest rates go up, bond prices go down; when interest rates go down, bond prices go up.

Here is a simple example. A $1,000 nominal value bond has a 5% coupon, is trading at $1,000, and is to be redeemed in one year's time, providing a redemption yield of 5% (note there is no capital gain). Now, suppose that interest rates go up to 10%. If this should happen, nobody will be willing to pay $1,000 for a fixed interest of $50. The price of the bond will need to fall, because investors are now expecting to earn 10% per annum. Indeed, it would need to fall to $954.54, as at this price the purchaser will still get a $50 coupon plus a capital gain of $45.46 in one year's time when the bond is redeemed for $1,000. This would result in a total return of $95.46 being achieved on an investment of $954.54, thereby providing a redemption yield of 10%. It is this piece of logic that results in bond prices falling when interest rates go up. Exactly the opposite happens when interest rates go down: bond prices go up.

It follows that bond prices are sensitive to any perceived changes in interest rates. Just how sensitive they are will be determined by two factors: the outstanding term to redemption and the coupon. The further away the redemption date is, the more sensitive the price will be to interest rate changes. Also, the lower the coupon, the more sensitive the price becomes.

This provides an opportunity for speculation. If you believe that interest rates are going to go down, you could capitalize on this by investing in bonds with a long term to redemption and/or a low coupon. You will still receive the coupon, plus you could potentially sell the bonds prior to redemption at a profit. Bear in mind that this essentially is gambling. A major US bank made global news when one of its traders lost billions of dollars on bonds by misreading what he thought was going to happen to interest rates. It must be emphasized that all of this is only relevant if you anticipate selling the bond prior to the redemption date. If you intend holding the bond for the full term, what happens to interest rates in the meantime is academic.

The other significant risk is default, the possibility that the issuer might default on interest payments and/or the repayment of the debt. Just as you can have a personal credit rating that assesses your ability to service and repay your debts, so bond issuers can have a **credit rating** that assesses their ability to service and repay their debts. There are three major agencies that issue government and corporate credit ratings:

* Standard & Poor's.
* Moody's.
* Fitch Ratings.

The best rating is known as triple A, which indicates the highest possible capacity to meet financial commitments. Thereafter, designations to indicate potential levels of default risk differ. Standard and Poor's and Fitch Ratings use a similar scale, with the lowest rating available being D. Moody's uses a different scale where the lowest rating available is C. In both instances, such a rating indicates

STANDARD & POOR'S/FITCH RATINGS	MOODY'S	
AAA	Aaa	
AA	Aa	Investment
A	A	grade ratings
BBB	Baa	
BB	Ba	
B	B	
CCC	Caa	Speculative
CC	Ca	grade ratings
C		
D	C	

GOVERNMENT AND CORPORATE CREDIT RATINGS

that default has occurred. The table above compares the main ratings used.

The top four ratings are commonly referred to as investment grade. Investors looking for low-risk opportunities will tend to restrict themselves to bonds with these ratings. The remaining ratings are known as speculative (or non-investment) grade. The latter tend to offer higher annual rates of return, but the risk of default increases as well. Sometimes these are referred to as junk bonds, which certainly does not mean that they are valueless, though the expression does emphasize that the level of risk is increased.

Standard & Poor's and Fitch Ratings sometimes attach a "+" or "-" sign to create additional subcategories of rating. For example, the AA rating comprises three subcategories, AA+, AA, and AA-, with AA+ being the highest and AA- the lowest. Moody's does something similar but using numbers. For example, its Aa rating can be divided into Aa1, Aa2, and Aa3, with Aa1 being the highest of the three ratings and Aa3 the lowest.

GROW YOUR OWN MONEY
If available, always check the credit rating of a bond issuer.

Credit rating information is readily available on many investment websites or by registering online directly with one of the agencies. Do bear in mind that a credit rating is only commenting on one aspect of bond risk – the risk of default. It does not comment on other risks such as bond prices moving due to interest rate changes. Also there is a potential problem when looking specifically at bonds issued by companies: not all companies have a credit rating. If this should be the case for a potential bond investment, you will need to look at other available data that may help you assess the financial stability of the issuer, such as trading results and news stories.

Stage 4 – Research

When it comes to liquidity, selling bonds is not usually a problem; you might receive more or less than you paid for them, but at least you will have access to your cash.

Term is a significant issue, however, when it comes to assessing the suitability of bonds. You can only guarantee the redemption yield if you hold the bond to the redemption date, so it is at this point that you need to make a decision. Are you investing for a specific event or are you more interested in developing a long-term reliable income stream? If you need cash at a specific point in the future, you should select bonds with maturities close to the desired date. If you want a regular income, you may be able to take advantage of the usually higher rates of return available on longer-term bonds. When adopting this latter strategy, a popular approach is to build what is called a **bond ladder**. This involves buying bonds with a variety of maturities, ranging from short to long.

Suppose that you have $20,000 available to invest. A bond ladder advocates that you spread this sum over several bonds with varying maturities. So you might invest $2,000 in bonds that mature in one year's time; another $2,000 in bonds that mature in two years' time; another $2,000 in bonds that mature in three years' time; and so on. That means that in a year's time $2,000 worth of bonds will mature, providing funds that you can use to buy bonds that will mature in another ten years' time. A year later a further $2,000 worth of bonds will mature, providing funds that you can use to invest in another tranche of bonds that will mature ten years thereafter. This will occur every year. Such a strategy allows you to take advantage of the higher rates of return typically associated with longer-term bonds while also ensuring that every year an issue is maturing, providing you with a healthy cash flow should you need it.

Unless you happen to be investing for a specific event, creating a bond ladder addresses the problems often associated with holding bonds that all have the same maturity date. If you only hold short-term bonds and then interest rates drop, you will be in a situation where you will have all your bonds maturing at the same time and the rates you will receive on any new bonds will be lower than were previously available. At the other end of the spectrum, if you hold only long-term bonds and interest rates rise, you will not have any bonds maturing and will therefore be unable to take advantage of the higher rates of return on offer.

In terms of capital, you need to check the minimum denomination. In the case of many corporate bonds, you should expect a minimum purchase requirement of at least $1,000.

Stage 5 – Review

Before you part with your money, review what you have found out in Stages 1 to 4:

* What is the redemption yield?
* Are there any unusual terms relating to this bond issue that need to be taken into account?
* Is it likely that the redemption yield will beat inflation?
* What is the likelihood of having to sell the bond prior to the redemption date?
* What is the issuer's credit rating?
* For how long are you prepared to tie up your money?
* Would the creation of a bond ladder be appropriate?
* What is the minimum investment?

Taking all of these factors into consideration, you can now decide whether or not you have found a home for your money.

Stage 6 – Revisit

Check the bonds in your portfolio every month or two. See if the credit ratings of any issuers have been downgraded, as this would indicate an increased risk of default.

In addition, if any bonds are close to their redemption date, decide what you intend to do with the proceeds. Are they to be used for a specific event or purchase, or do you intend to reinvest? If you are keen to achieve a capital gain, have bond prices gone up?

THE ESSENTIALS
* **RECOGNIZE** – find a bond that appeals. The higher the risk and/or the longer the term to redemption, the higher the rate of return on offer tends to be.
* **REWARD** – check the redemption yield.
* **RISK** – check the issuer's credit rating to assess the risk of default. If you intend to sell before the redemption date, consider the impact of interest rate changes. Other risks to be taken into account are inflation and issue conditions, along with supply and demand on the day.
* **RESEARCH** – check term and capital. Confirm the redemption date and the minimum investment. Consider whether a bond ladder would be appropriate to your needs.
* **REVIEW** – based on what you now know, does this bond meet your requirements?
* **REVISIT** – remain vigilant. Keep watching the performance of your portfolio and review relevant credit ratings.

7

FIGURING IT OUT:

INVESTING IN SHARES 1

Although both savings accounts and bonds are wealth-creating assets, it's unlikely you're going to meet anybody who made their fortune from them. If you want to grow your wealth to any significant degree, there are two types of wealth-creating asset to consider: shares and property. As property demands significant investment from the outset, for many people the more accessible option is shares (which are also called stocks), whether it be through direct purchase or through some form of managed fund. The problem with using a managed fund is that the fees can be considerable, often amounting to tens of thousands of dollars over a typical investor's lifetime. Taking control and making your own investment decisions, rather than relying on an anonymous third party to make your decisions for you, can save you a small fortune in fees. Because of their popularity, their potential for growing your money significantly, and the opportunity to avoid paying onerous fees, shares enjoy the honor of having not one, but two chapters dedicated to them.

When opening a savings account, you know in advance what rate of interest you are going to achieve and, should it alter in the future, you reserve the right to withdraw your funds. In the case of bonds, you know exactly how much interest you are going to earn and for how long.

You also know exactly how much you will receive back at the end of the term. By contrast, in the case of shares, you do not know how much you are going to earn and there is no guarantee you will ever get your money back. Not surprisingly, then, the practicalities of this particular form of wealth-creating asset are a little more involved than the other forms of investment covered in this book, but don't let this put you off.

The main barrier to be overcome if you want to invest in shares is not technical, it's psychological. The real problem when it comes to share dealing is not that it's complex (it isn't), it's the fact that people *believe* it's complex. In the next two chapters we're going to discover that investing in shares is well within the capabilities of the average person on the street. Over the years I've encountered many aspiring investors who finally took the plunge and started to deal in shares on their own account. The reaction has nearly always been the same: "Why didn't I start doing this years ago?"

When you break share dealing down into its core elements, there really is precious little mystery to this particular form of investment. All you're looking for is a healthy return on your cash. In order to achieve this there are two hurdles that need to be overcome:

* You need to confirm that the company is well managed.
* You need to ensure that you are paying a fair price for the shares.

Satisfy yourself on both of these issues and you're well on your way to achieving a decent rate of return. I should emphasize that it is essential you address both issues: too many people focus on one or the other. For example, some investors believe that share dealing is all about identifying well-managed businesses; regrettably, if you overpay for the shares, that will erode your overall rate of return, regardless of how the business is performing. As I often say to delegates, investing in overpriced shares is no different to investing in a poorly managed company – both will produce lousy returns.

The focus of this chapter is on assessing how effectively a company is being managed and thereby identifying its strengths and weaknesses. Most importantly, we're going to find out how this can be done quickly – literally in a matter of minutes. In Chapter 8 we're going to build on this understanding to determine whether or not the share price represents a good-value, long-term investment opportunity.

Making profit is a process

When you're investing in shares, you're investing in a business, so a prerequisite to being a successful independent investor is the ability to make sense of the trading results – to understand the figures. Too many people invest in shares because a colleague has given them a hot tip, only to watch their investment subsequently plunge in value. Would you buy a car without seeing it first? Of course not; you'd want to look it over to check it's okay. So why would you buy a share without first looking over the company? My view is that a hot tip is a sure way of getting burned.

If you scour the internet, you will find vast amounts of information about company performance. If you were to collate all the data available for a single company, it could take you days, even weeks, to work through it. The trouble is that by the time you've done this, the world will have moved on and there will be more news stories, trading updates, and so on. It's for this very reason that many people are prepared to hand over their money to fund managers and let them do the research; it's all too time consuming. What you're going to discover in this chapter is a fast means of assessing whether or not a company offers investment potential.

Over the years I have developed a skill set that enables me to climb inside a company's trading results very quickly. When I'm giving a presentation on share dealing, I sometimes set the audience the challenge of giving me a full set of trading results for any company of their choosing. Within one minute, I guarantee I'll be able to say whether the company is doing well or is struggling. Give me five minutes and I will have identified all its strengths and weaknesses as well. That might sound impressive – or even boastful – but in this chapter I'm going to show you how to do just that.

Let's start with why companies exist in the first place. The primary commercial objective, and this is why shareholders are prepared to invest in them, is to generate profit. But what is profit? In a business context, profit measures changes in wealth. When a business says that it made a profit last year, what it's really saying is that its wealth has increased – it owns more. That is why losses are such bad news: investors are literally being told that their wealth has gone down.

Once a year every company is obliged to produce a document called an **annual report**. In essence this report says to the shareholders: "You've given us your money. Let us show you what we've done with it." This is the single

most important document you can access if you want to
assess how a company is being managed; that is, whether
or not it's being run on a profitable basis. Although quarterly or half-yearly updates are not uncommon, the most
important results are the annual figures. These reports typically range from about 20 pages up to 200 pages or more,
which is a lot of information to take in. And then there are
the figures, quite often hundreds if not thousands of them.
How on earth can you hope to fight your way through all
of this?

There are many books on how to read and interpret
annual reports. Most of them are technical, resorting to all
sorts of devious numerical manipulations. Even given my
financial background, I often find I'm losing the will to live
when reading through one of these tomes. The most common approach they advocate when analyzing an annual
report is to view making profit as a jigsaw. There are many
pieces, but if you're able to fit them all together, you'll be
able to see the complete picture; which is fine if you're tech-
nically minded, but it really does take a long time. It also
has the downside that if you happen to miss out on any of
the pieces, you may end up seeing the wrong picture.

I disagree with the jigsaw analogy. To me, making
profit is a process that starts when shareholders invest
money and finishes when the company says that it has
made a profit. Indeed, much of the work I do with corporate clients is explaining how the profit-making process
works and, most importantly, helping them identify what
practical steps they can take to improve it. So this is not
a theory, this is the real world. What is of particular rele-
vance here is that, from your point of view as an investor,
by understanding the process you can readily identify the
strengths and weaknesses of any company. This in turn

will help you assess whether or not any business provides an attractive investment opportunity.

Measuring business success

We know that investors are motivated by rate of return. I get very frustrated when companies simply report their profit figures. If a company says that it made $15 million profit last year, how can you say it's doing well or it's doing badly if you haven't got a clue how much shareholders had to invest in that business in the first place? If it turns out that the shareholders originally invested $1,500 million, I would suggest that it is not doing very well at all.

To overcome this problem, shareholders have a measure that is equivalent to the rate of interest quoted on a savings account – **return on equity**. This looks at the profit a business earns as a percentage of the funds invested. Don't be put off by the title; return is just another word for profit and equity is an alternative word for the owners' stake.

KEY MEASURE

$$\text{Return on equity} = \frac{\textbf{Profit}}{\textbf{Shareholders' funds}} \times 100\%$$

If shareholders have $100 million invested in a company that generates an annual profit of $10 million, the return on equity is 10%. The higher the percentage, the more effectively shareholders' funds are being utilized.

GROW YOUR OWN MONEY
Always check the return on equity to assess how effectively a company is being managed.

What is a reasonable return on equity? The most effective way to answer this question is to look at what companies themselves believe they should be able to achieve.
Unfortunately, the only way to find this out is to get inside
the companies and ask the boards of directors; not an easy
thing to do for an average member of the public. I have
been in the privileged position of having worked with
many companies over the years and there is a generally
accepted minimum rate of return that is targeted by most
of them. Ironically, this minimum is not based on numbers; it is based on logic. Most companies agree that the
minimum acceptable rate of return should be at least double the long-term "risk-free" rate of return achievable on
cash deposits.

When someone is considering investing in a company, they have a choice. They could buy the shares or they
could put their money in a savings account. Because shares
are usually regarded as a long-term investment, logically
the returns to be achieved on those funds ought to be
compared with rates achievable in the long term on cash
deposits. Short-term movements in interest rates are of no
interest here; it is what people are expecting to earn on
cash deposits over several years that counts.

Suppose that you could earn 5% per annum by simply investing in a savings account. Because shares are more
risky, you would obviously want a higher rate of return
than this to compensate for the increased risk. Companies
take the view that you would probably want at least to
double this rate as a minimum to entice you to part with
your money. On this basis, they would endeavor to deliver
at least a 10% return on equity per annum. This is not science; this is pure intuition.

QUICK CHALLENGE

You are invited to invest in a new business venture and you are warned that if things go wrong you could lose your entire investment; but if things go well, you will receive 1% above your current savings rate. How do you feel about this as a business proposal?

Like most people, you would probably walk away from the deal. However, if you were told that there was an opportunity to double your rate of return, maybe even treble it, now it might well start to get your attention. This is the logic employed in the corporate world. If a company can't at least double the risk-free rate of return, why would anybody want to invest in it?

I should emphasize that this is a *minimum* rate of return. Many companies will strive to achieve rates of return significantly higher than this.

A persistent low-inflation environment in most major economies has resulted in return on equity expectations remaining reasonably unchanged for many years. Taking this into account, coupled with my experience working with companies from around the globe, the following table provides a broad-brush approach to interpreting return on equity figures:

VALUE	INTERPRETATION
Less than 10%	Low rate of return
10% to 20%	Reasonable rate of return
Over 20%	High rate of return

INTERPRETING RETURN ON EQUITY

What return on equity is actually doing is summarizing how effective the management team is at managing the profit-making process.

Profit

The process finishes with a profit being made

Return on equity = ————————————— x 100%

Shareholders' funds

The process starts with funds being invested

RETURN ON EQUITY SUMMARIZES THE
PROFIT-MAKING PROCESS

Like any process, profit-making can be broken down into stages and in this instance there are three. The really good news is that the stages are the same for every type of company, regardless of whether it's a retailer, a car manufacturer, an oil exploration business, or whatever. To understand what the three stages are, we need to start at the beginning of the process with shareholders' funds.

The first stage of the profit-making process

It is a commonly held view that companies need shareholders to provide the funds they require to trade, but this is not true. Companies need shareholders for a very specific purpose and if you are considering buying shares in a company, it is essential that you understand what that purpose is.

One way to appreciate the role of shareholders is to examine a business that does not need any shareholders at all. Suppose that, with all the talk of global warming in the news, you have decided that the up-and-coming product is umbrellas. Whether they're to protect from the rain or from the sun, umbrellas are the future. You set up a website where you take customers' orders, your trading terms are payment with order, and you promise to ship the umbrellas as soon as they are in stock. In your first month of trading you receive $2,500 worth of orders. You then go to a supplier and pay him $2,000 to fulfill your orders, which leaves you with $500 profit. That is all that happens during the first month.

Now comes the critical question: How much money did you have to invest to start the business off? As it turns out, you didn't have to invest anything at all. Well done – you've created a business that needs no investment whatsoever. But how did you do that? The business did indeed need funds to operate but, by insisting that your customers paid you in advance, you got the required funds from them; no investors required.

Now let's revisit this umbrella business, but with one alteration – we're going to change the timings. Instead of collecting money from customers at the outset, you decide to buy the umbrellas from the supplier first. As previously, they cost you $2,000. Also as previously, you sell them for $2,500. Although the profit remains at $500, something has changed. In this second scenario you need to invest $2,000 at the outset to finance the umbrellas. In this business umbrellas are inventory and inventory is a form of asset (it is something the business owns). This is why companies need shareholders: to finance assets. Other types of asset that you might find in a business include buildings, equipment, furniture, and vehicles, all of which need to be financed.

The fact that shareholders' funds are needed to finance assets raises a question. Where does the money come from to pay the recurring expenses like payroll, utility bills, and so on? The point to note here is that sales pay the day-to-day expenses, so there are two cash streams into every company: shareholders provide the cash needed to finance the assets, while sales provide the cash needed to pay for the day-to-day expenses.

Although we have established that shareholders are needed to finance assets, there is another source of finance available: companies can borrow the money. This might be achieved through a conventional bank loan, through the issue of bonds, or simply by obtaining credit from suppliers. This in itself creates a dilemma: Is it preferable to raise money from shareholders or to borrow it? If a company doesn't make any profit, it doesn't have to pay investors a dividend. Of course, if the business is profitable, paying investors shouldn't be a problem. By contrast, if a company borrows money, it is obliged to pay any interest due regardless of how the business is doing. This would seem to suggest that companies should always endeavor to raise funds from shareholders. Despite the appeal of this argument, many companies are saddled with huge amounts of debt. Nobody told them they had to do this; they went into debt totally voluntarily. But why would any business want to operate this way?

At a personal level, you may well dream of the day you finally pay off all those debts – the mortgage, the car loan, and the credit cards. In the corporate world many companies would argue that you're crazy to think this way: you ought to be thinking about how to get into debt, not how to get out of it. Believe it or not, many businesses love debt, and the reason they love it is because it can help improve return on equity. Strange as it may sound, in the business world debt can be your best friend. Let me explain how this works.

If we return to the latest version of your umbrella business, where you needed to invest $2,000 to finance inventory that you subsequently sold for $2,500, providing a profit of $500, in this instance your return on equity is 25% ($500 profit as a percentage of the $2,000 investment). Suppose that, in addition to your $2,000 investment, you decide to take out a bank loan for $2,000. Now you can buy $4,000 worth of umbrellas. No doubt you can spot an advantage of borrowing already: you can spend so much more! In the previous scenario, when you bought umbrellas for $2,000, you were able to sell them for $2,500. It follows that, if you can now buy $4,000 worth of umbrellas, you should be able to sell these for $5,000.

The problem with borrowing money, of course, is that you have to pay interest. If you are being charged 10% on the loan, out of the $1,000 you are now making from buying and selling the umbrellas, you have to pay the bank $200 interest (10% of the $2,000 loan). Your profit will fall to $800, but now comes the exquisite twist. How much of your money have you invested in this venture? The answer is still $2,000. That means that you have made $800 profit on a $2,000 investment, giving you a 40% return on equity. You have increased your rate of return from 25% to 40% and all you have done is borrowed money.

It is often argued that another problem with borrowing money, in addition to having to pay interest, is that you have to pay the loan back. Ironically, for many companies paying off a loan is not perceived as a problem – in fact, they have no intention of ever paying it off. Indeed, many businesses regard loans as a permanent facility, and there is a logic behind this.

We've just established that by borrowing money, the return to shareholders can be increased. This suggests that if a loan was paid off, the company's rate of return could drop. Shareholders wouldn't feel particularly happy about that. Nor would the bank, because it only earns interest while the money is being borrowed. So by paying off a loan, a company could end up upsetting both its shareholders and its bank. Why upset people? Don't pay off the loan, then everyone's happy!

Based on the discussion so far it might appear that if a company wants to be successful, all it has to do is borrow lots of money, but the situation is not quite that straightforward. Things can go wrong. By assuming debt companies are also assuming risk, the most critical of which regards sales. What happens if the company fails to make its budgeted sales figure? Everything rotates around this number.

Returning to the latest scenario of your umbrella business, suppose that your sales are not $5,000; they come in at $4,700. In this instance you will be making $700 buying and selling umbrellas ($4,700 sales less $4,000 spent on the inventory), out of which $200 interest needs to be paid to the bank. This would result in your profit dropping to the original $500. It follows that if your business comes in more than $300 below the sales plan of $5,000 (which is only a 6% drop), you will end up achieving a return on equity that is lower than it would have been if you had only achieved $2,500 worth of sales with no borrowing at all. That is the risk.

This is a valuable lesson. Borrowing funds can benefit companies that are able to deliver robust sales each year, but it can cause serious problems for businesses whose sales performance is more erratic. Of course, not all

borrowed funds are necessarily subject to interest charges
– a company might obtain 60 days' credit from its suppliers, for instance. No interest is typically applicable in
this situation, but there is still risk involved. The company
could become reliant on the continuing existence of that
credit facility to trade effectively in the future, so that if the
credit should ever be withdrawn, it might struggle. Thus
borrowing money, regardless of whether interest is payable
or not, exposes a company to risk.

Shareholders' FUNDS   **and/or**   **Borrowed FUNDS**
are required to finance
ASSETS

THE FIRST STAGE OF THE PROFIT-MAKING PROCESS

This is the first stage of the profit-making process: companies need to raise funds (from shareholders or in the form of
loans) to finance assets. It follows that when assessing how
effectively a company is managing the profit-making process,
this is the first issue that needs to be addressed. Fortunately,
there is a measure that can assist, called **gearing** (or lever-
age). This states the proportion of funds raised by a business
that have been borrowed. Having identified a company's
return on equity, gearing is always the next thing I look at.

There are a variety of ways of working this figure out;
some are quite technical, others less so. I like to keep

things as simple as possible, so I use a very straightforward calculation. I simply take total borrowed funds as a percentage of total assets.

KEY MEASURE

$$\text{Gearing} = \frac{\textbf{Borrowed funds}}{\textbf{Assets}} \times 100\%$$

Many accountants would probably suffer apoplexy if they saw the gearing calculation above. They would no doubt wax lyrical about "non-interest-bearing liabilities needing to be excluded from the computation" and other equally exciting technicalities. That is not the issue here; all we are trying to do is assess how the business is being managed and for this purpose the calculation works just fine.

In the latest scenario of your umbrella business, you acquire $4,000 worth of umbrellas (assets), of which $2,000 worth is financed by borrowings:

$$\text{Gearing} = \frac{\textbf{Borrowed funds of \$2,000}}{\textbf{Assets of \$4,000}} \times 100\%$$

$$= \ 50\%$$

A gearing of 50% tells us that half of all funds raised to finance assets are borrowed.

It is time for a bit of jargon. If the majority of funds raised are borrowed (i.e., gearing is over 50%), a company is said to be high geared. If the majority of funds raised are from shareholders (i.e., gearing is less than 50%), it is said to be low geared. When the split is 50-50, it is gearing neutral.

Low-geared companies do not tend to raise any alarm bells, as the nature of their funding is indicative of low interest commitments and/or a low reliance on third-party credit. By contrast, high-geared companies warrant further investigation. The attraction of high gearing is that it can result in increased rates of return for shareholders, but this is a situation where you need to study the company's sales performance. Provided that the company is delivering robust sales each year, the high gearing may well not be a problem, but if sales are erratic, there could be trading problems ahead: it may be unable to meet its interest commitments and/or credit facilities may be withdrawn.

The second stage of the profit-making process

Given that the first stage of the profit-making process involves raising funds to finance assets, this leads on to the next question: Why do companies need assets? For example, why do retail businesses want stores and inventory? The answer is to generate sales.

ASSETS
are required to generate
SALES

THE SECOND STAGE OF THE PROFIT-MAKING PROCESS

Asset turnover looks at how effectively a company is utilizing its assets to generate sales and is worked out by dividing sales by assets. This is always the next figure I look at, after gearing.

KEY MEASURE

$$\text{Asset turnover} = \frac{\text{Sales}}{\text{Assets}}$$

In the latest scenario of your umbrella business, you invested $4,000 in assets (umbrellas) and produced sales of $5,000.

$$\text{Asset turnover} = \frac{\text{Sales of } \$5,000}{\text{Assets of } \$4,000}$$

$$= 1.25$$

This says that from every $1 you invest in assets, you produce $1.25 worth of sales: the higher the number, the more effectively you are managing your assets and the higher your return on equity should be.

Don't underestimate the importance of asset turnover. Once funds have been raised to finance assets, the only source of cash available to a business is sales. We have already noted that you need sales to pay day-to-day expenses so, not surprisingly, there is a link between asset turnover and cost management. If a company has a low asset turnover, the cash generation from its assets is low, which means that it needs to keep a very tight rein on costs. However, if a company has a high asset turnover, it is generating far more cash from its assets, allowing it to spend more on the product offer, marketing, staffing, and so on. Without a healthy asset turnover, it is impossible to run a profitable business.

The third stage of the profit-making process

If the second stage of the profit-making process is all about turning assets into sales, this leads on to yet another question: Why does any business want sales? The answer, of course, is to make profit. This is the third and indeed final stage of the process: turning sales into profit.

SALES
are required to generate
PROFIT

THE THIRD STAGE OF THE PROFIT-MAKING PROCESS

To assess how effectively the third stage of the process is being managed, once again there is a measure that comes to our rescue. **Profit margin** looks at profit as a percentage of sales.

KEY MEASURE

$$\text{Profit margin} = \frac{\text{Profit}}{\text{Sales}} \times 100\%$$

Let's stay with the latest scenario for your umbrella business, where you bought umbrellas for $4,000 and sold them for $5,000. Out of that $1,000 gain you paid $200 in interest, leaving you with a profit of $800.

$$\text{Profit margin} = \frac{\text{Profit of } \$800}{\text{Sales of } \$5,000} \times 100\%$$

$$= 16\%$$

A profit margin of 16% tells us that, out of every $1 sale, 16 cents is profit; the bigger the percentage, the better you are doing. What profit margin is really commenting on, though, is your cost management. If you are making 16 cents in the dollar, it follows that you must be spending 84 cents. If you can spend less than 84 cents you have improved your profit margin, which in turn will improve your return on equity.

Note that the objective of cost management in a business is not to minimize costs. The objective is to minimize costs as a percentage of sales, as this will maximize the profit margin, which will in turn help maximize the return on equity.

Suppose that a company enjoys an annual turnover of $100 million and spends $10 million on payroll, so that its payroll is running at 10% of sales. If it can reduce payroll as a percentage of sales, the profit margin will improve. It does not follow that, in order to achieve this, the company needs to get rid of staff. One way to reduce the percentage is to make sure that as sales increase, the payroll bill grows at a slower rate. If this can be achieved, though expenditure on payroll might be increasing, as a percentage of sales the cost will have reduced and that is what counts. Indeed, sometimes getting rid of staff might be the worst thing to do if it results in falling sales. The objective of cost management is to *maximize productivity*: to ensure that, on every dollar a company spends, it is generating the highest possible level of sales.

Understanding the objective of cost management can prove particularly useful when companies announce a new cost initiative. Are they announcing an initiative that would make them more cost efficient, which could potentially improve return on equity, or are they announcing a straightforward cost-cutting exercise, which could end up damaging sales and, by association, return on equity?

The four-figure trick

So profit-making is a three-stage process:

* Stage 1 – raising funds to finance assets.
* Stage 2 – turning assets into sales.
* Stage 3 – turning sales into profit.

These three stages combined determine a company's return on equity. For a potential investor, the real benefit of understanding this process is that it enables you to climb inside a business quickly.

At this juncture it would not surprise me if you were thinking, even though this might all appear highly relevant, "How could I ever be expected to find the time to put this into practice?" Now here's the remarkable thing. One of the objectives of this book is to identify shortcuts: fast ways of accessing the information that you need to make a decision. What I am about to show you is one of the most

Shareholders' FUNDS   and/or   **Borrowed FUNDS**

are required to finance

ASSETS

which are required to generate

SALES

which are required to generate

PROFIT

THE COMPLETE PROFIT-MAKING PROCESS

powerful shortcuts I know. I devised it many years ago and I call it the "four-figure trick," not because it's a trick or an illusion, but because its simplicity can really take people by surprise when they encounter it for the first time.

We have been introduced to four measures in this chapter:

* Return on equity.
* Gearing.

* Asset turnover.
* Profit margin.

The good news is that in order to work out all four of these measures, you just need to extract four figures from the annual report:

* Sales.
* Total assets.
* Net profit.
* Shareholders' funds.

Within the annual report are two very important financial statements: the balance sheet and the **income statement** (or profit and loss account). A company balance sheet is similar to a personal balance sheet. It adds up what the company owns (its assets) and deducts what it owes (its liabilities) in order to identify what it is worth (its wealth) at a specific point in time. An income statement, by contrast, tells you how that wealth has altered over time; it tells you whether the company's wealth is going up (it has made a profit) or going down (it has made a loss).

It is important to appreciate exactly what these two financial statements are saying:

* A balance sheet says what a company is worth *at the end of the year*.
* An income statement says how much profit has been made *during the year*.

Summary statements for Spotter Gooden are shown overleaf.

When looking at live financial statements, the only difference will be the level of detail. In practice, you will find a detailed analysis of assets, liabilities, sales, and costs. All we are interested in here, for the purposes of analyzing performance, are the totals.

SPOTTER GOODEN FINANCIAL STATEMENTS
Balance sheet ($m)

Assets	50
Liabilities	−30
Shareholders' funds	20

Income statement ($m)

Sales	80
Costs	−76
Net income	4

Spotter Gooden has assets (such as property, equipment, vehicles, and so forth) worth $50 million and liabilities (amounts owed to suppliers, employees, banks, the government, and so forth) worth $30 million. This means, in theory at least, that the company could be closed down tomorrow, sell off everything it owns, pay off everything it owes, and still be left with $20 million in the bank. This is shareholders' money. So the balance sheet is telling us that shareholders have $20 million physically invested in the business. This is called the **book value** of the company or its net asset value.

It is not uncommon for the book value to be used as a proxy for the breakup value of the business. In reality this may not always be true, as the values quoted on a balance sheet sometimes bear little relationship to what the assets would be sold for if they had to be disposed of at short notice. If a car manufacturer bought some custom-made equipment for $60 million to produce components that were unique to its vehicles, it would argue that it has just acquired $60 million worth of assets. The secondhand value, though, might only be a few thousand dollars as, being custom built, this equipment would not be of any use to another car manufacturer.

Turning our attention to the income statement, although it may look complex when you look at one for real, the core elements are easy to understand. It deducts the company's costs from its sales in order to identify how much profit has been made. Spotter Gooden has generated sales of $80 million, out of which it has had to pay costs of $76 million (such as employee costs, property costs, taxes, and so forth), leaving it with a profit of $4 million.

Regrettably, companies have a habit of confusing people by bombarding them with lots of different profit figures. They talk about gross profit, trading profit, underlying profit, pre-tax profit, and so the list continues. The main profit figure that a shareholder cares about is called the profit after tax or net income. This simply refers to the profit a company has made after it has paid everybody, including the government. It is like your pay. Your gross pay is of interest to you, but what counts is your net pay – the pay you are left with after paying tax to the government. That is the money that you can do with as you see fit. So it is with companies. What concerns shareholders is the profit a company achieves after it has paid its tax bill, as that is the profit available for them. This is usually the last figure shown on an income statement and it can enjoy a variety of titles, such as "net income," "net profit," or "profit available to equity shareholders," to name but a few.

Given that profit measures changes in wealth, Spotter Gooden's income statement tells us that the company has increased its wealth (in terms of what it owns and owes)

by $4 million. But is $4 million a good or a bad level of
profit? What we want to determine is how the business
is performing. How effectively is it managing the profit-
making process?

It is time to do a few brief calculations. The first step
is to extract the relevant information from the annual
report. Let's revisit the two financial statements for Spotter
Gooden, this time highlighting the information required.

SPOTTER GOODEN FINANCIAL STATEMENTS
Balance sheet ($m)

Assets	**50**
Liabilities	**−30**
Shareholders' funds	**20**

Income statement ($m)

Sales	**80**
Costs	**−76**
Net income	**4**

All that you need to do is jot down just four figures:

* Assets of $50 million.
* Shareholders' funds of $20 million.
* Sales of $80 million.
* Net income (profit) of $4 million.

This is all the information you need to establish the company's return on equity, gearing, asset turnover, and profit
margin. I should emphasize that the answers you will get
will be approximations, but for the purposes of assessing how the business is being managed, that is all that is
required. If you want to obtain more precise results, this

can be readily achieved, but it does require a little more work.

The challenge relates to the figures being extracted specifically from the balance sheet, as this document only provides a snapshot of the company at the end of the trading year. Why is this an issue? Take return on equity as a case in point. To calculate this, you look at profit as a percentage of the shareholders' funds invested in the business. If you do this utilizing the figures we have just extracted for Spotter Gooden, you will be looking at the profit achieved during the year as a percentage of the shareholders' funds invested at the end of the year. Provided that shareholders' funds have not altered too much during the 12-month period, this will provide a reasonable approximation, but the answer will not be precise.

QUICK CHALLENGE

You have earned $100 interest on a savings account during the last year, but you want to work out your rate of return. What other figure would you need to know in order to do this?

To work out the rate of return, you don't need to know how much was in the account at the end of the year, but rather the average balance during the year. It's the same with return on equity. If you want to work out an accurate figure, you need to know the average value of shareholders' funds during the year. This can be easily established from a company's reported balance sheet, because it will always provide values at the end of the current year and (for comparison purposes) at the end of the previous year. To obtain an average value, you add the two figures together and divide by two. The same approach would need to be adopted for assets, as this figure also comes from the balance sheet. The good news is that you don't need to average the figures extracted from the income statement as, by its very nature, this document tells you what has happened during the year.

So you have a choice. If you are happy to work with approximate values, all you need to extract from the annual report are four figures, exactly as you see them:

* Assets.
* Shareholders' funds.
* Sales.
* Net income.

If you want more accurate results, you still extract the two figures from the income statement, exactly as you see them:

* Sales.
* Net income.

But then you must calculate the following two figures, based on the values reported in the balance sheet:

* Average assets.
* Average shareholders' funds.

As soon as you have done this, you can put the annual report to one side; you don't need it any more. For the remainder of this chapter, we are going to stick with the most straightforward approach, using the four figures exactly as we see them (no averaging).

Having extracted the relevant figures, the next step is to see how the company has been doing overall. Return on equity tells us how effectively a business converts share-holders' funds into profit:

$$\text{Return on equity} = \frac{\text{Profit of \$4 million}}{\text{Shareholders' funds of \$20 million}} \times 100\%$$

$$= 20\%$$

This tells us that, on every $100 invested by sharehold-ers, the company generates a profit of $20. What we now want to understand is how it achieved this. In order to do that, we need to examine how it has been managing the profit-making process itself.

We know that the first stage of the profit-making pro-cess involves raising funds to finance assets and that gear-ing tells us what proportion of funds raised is borrowed. We have noted that the assets of Spotter Gooden total $50 million and that $20 million worth is being financed by shareholders' funds. This means that the company must be borrowing the difference, $30 million. You may be think-ing that you can see liabilities on the balance sheet totaling $30 million anyway, so why didn't we just jot down that number as well? We could have done, but my philosophy is why write down five numbers when you only need four? By combining the borrowed funds figure with the assets figure we can calculate the gearing:

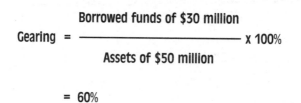

$$\text{Gearing} = \frac{\text{Borrowed funds of \$30 million}}{\text{Assets of \$50 million}} \times 100\%$$

$$= 60\%$$

Out of every $100 of funds raised, $60 is borrowed. This incorporates all sources of finance (with the exception of shareholders) and would include amounts owed to suppliers, the government, banks, and so on. Remember, the higher the gearing, the more reliant the company is on generating sufficient sales to meet its interest commitments and/or the more reliant it is on third-party credit.

The second stage of the profit-making process involves turning assets into sales. Asset turnover tells us how effective a business is at doing this:

$$\text{Asset turnover} = \frac{\text{Sales of \$80m}}{\text{Assets of \$50m}}$$

$$= 1.6$$

From every $1 Spotter Gooden has invested in assets, the business is producing sales of $1.60. The higher the figure, the more effectively the company is managing its assets.

The final stage of the profit-making process involves examining how effectively costs are being managed. The profit margin tells us how effective a business is at balancing its costs against sales to ensure that there is still a profit left at the end of the day:

$$\text{Profit margin} = \frac{\text{Profit of \$4 million}}{\text{Sales of \$80 million}} \times 100\%$$

$$= 5\%$$

In the case of Spotter Gooden, out of every $1 sale a profit of 5 cents is being delivered. In other words, the company is spending 95 cents to achieve every $1 sale. The higher the profit margin, the more effectively costs are being managed.

Now it is time to bring all these results together to provide a coherent picture of how this company is being managed. Breaking profit-making down into three distinct stages provides a fast and effective method for identifying how a company is delivering a return on shareholders' funds. This can be achieved by combining the four measures calculated above into an analytical tool that I have devised called a **return on equity flowchart**. Probably the easiest way to explain how it works is to show you the flowchart for Spotter Gooden and walk you through it, step by step.

This is a tool that has been developed to analyze any company quickly. The problem is that companies vary in size and we inevitably will want to be able to compare them. The easiest way to overcome this is to examine what happens to each $100 of funds raised. That way we can immediately compare a company that is raising billions of dollars with a company that is raising just a few million. The critical issue is which company will manage the $100 better.

The top of the flowchart starts by looking at what happens to a $100 tranche of funding. Spotter Gooden has gearing of 60%, which tells us that, out of every $100 being raised, $60 of it is borrowed, which means that the remaining $40 must be coming from the shareholders.

The reason that $100 is being raised of course is to finance $100 worth of assets. We now turn our attention to how those assets are performing. With an asset turnover of 1.6, we know that Spotter Gooden generates $1.60 worth of

Gearing is	60%
	⬇
For every $100 of funds raised...	
Shareholders provide	$40
Other sources provide	$60
	⬇
Which is used to finance...	
Assets worth	$100
	⬇
Asset turnover is	1.6
	⬇
So every $100 of assets generates...	
Sales of	$160
	⬇
Profit margin is	5%
	⬇
So the sales generate...	
Profit of	$8
	⬇
Which produces...	
Return on equity of	20%

RETURN ON EQUITY FLOWCHART

sales from every dollar of assets. It follows that, from every $100 worth of assets, sales of $160 are being generated.

The final stage of the profit-making process is to convert sales into profit. Spotter Gooden has a profit margin of 5%, which tells us that 5% of sales is profit. In this instance the sales figure is $160, 5% of which gives us a profit of $8.

We are now in a position to work out the return on equity. We have just established that, for every $100 of funds raised, shareholders are investing $40, on which a profit of $8 is being made, giving a return on equity of 20%.

On one page we can clearly see how this company has managed to deliver a 20% return on equity. Constructing a flowchart for the previous year and comparing the results will clearly highlight which aspects of the business are strengthening and/or which are weakening. I have been doing this for years and can do the whole analysis in five minutes flat. In fairness, I would not expect most people to be able to match that, but once you get used to doing the calculations, I reckon 15 minutes to complete the entire exercise would be realistic. Given that you may be considering putting your money into this business and you clearly do not want to make the wrong investment decision, I would argue that this is time well spent.

The entire process can be speeded up considerably if you are conversant with spreadsheets. By creating one that does the calculations for you, all you then have to do is to type in the four numbers from the annual report and you will see the flowchart immediately. Bear in mind that even in the absence of a spreadsheet, we are only talking about a few minutes of your time; probably not much longer than the time it takes to have a cup of tea (and you can always find time for a cup of tea).

Insight Investing provides a detailed weekly analysis of every major company traded on the London Stock Exchange, incorporating a return on equity flowchart. As can be seen from the example shown overleaf, once constructed, the flowchart provides a powerful overview of how a company is being managed.

TRADING PERFORMANCE

	ROE Flowchart		
Year ended	30/09/2013	30/09/2012	Comments
Gearing is	56.2%	60.1%	✖ Deterioration
	⬇	⬇	
For every £100 of funds raised...			
Shareholders provide	£43.77	£39.92	
Other sources provide	£56.23	£60.08	
	⬇	⬇	
Which is used to finance...			
Assets worth	£100.00	£100.00	
	⬇	⬇	
Asset turnover is	0.98	0.88	✔ Improvement
	⬇	⬇	
So every £100 of assets generates...			
Sales of	£97.81	£87.95	
	⬇	⬇	
Profit margin is	9.3%	6.6%	✔ Improvement
	⬇	⬇	
So the sales generate...			
Profit of	£9.14	£5.82	
	⬇	⬇	
Which produces...			
Return on equity of	**20.9%**	**14.6%**	✔ Improvement

INSIGHT INVESTING: ASSESSING TRADING PERFORMANCE

This analytical tool gets you to focus on the big issues that have an impact on the performance of every business:

* Gearing (how it raises funds).
* Asset turnover (its ability to use assets to generate sales).
* Profit margin (its ability to turn sales into profit).

Even if you don't have a great affinity with numbers, simply listening to or reading the news can provide valuable hints. Are there any indications that the company you are considering is about to increase (or reduce) its borrowing needs? Is there any suggestion that it is going to be utilizing its assets more or less effectively? Are there any indications that costs are likely to be managed more or less efficiently? Any such information will help you build a picture of the company's future trading potential.

Don't forget interest and dividends

In addition to the measures encapsulated within the profit-making process, there are two issues that can have an impact on the future viability of a company from an investor's point of view:

* Its ability to meet its future interest commitments.
* Its ability to maintain its dividend payments.

Interest cover states how many times profit covers interest payments.

KEY MEASURE

$$\text{Interest cover} = \frac{\text{Profit before interest payments}}{\text{Interest payable}}$$

If a company makes $10 million profit, out of which it has to pay interest of $2 million, the interest cover is 5. This says that the company is making five times more profit than it needs to pay out in interest on its loans. The higher the number, the less chance there is of the company being unable to meet its interest commitments in the future. Interest cover of 2 or more is normally deemed adequate for most investors.

Dividend cover states how many times profit covers dividends.

KEY MEASURE

$$\text{Dividend cover} = \frac{\text{Profit before dividend payments}}{\text{Dividends payable}}$$

This is similar to interest cover. If a company makes $6 million profit out of which it pays $2 million worth of dividends, the dividend cover is 3. This tells us that the company is making three times more profit than the dividends it pays out. The higher the number, the more likely it is that the company will be able to maintain dividend payments in the future. As with interest cover, a value of 2 or more is normally deemed adequate for most investors.

You do not need to worry too much about the intricacies of these calculations, such as where to find the profit before interest payments figure, as both interest cover and dividend cover are commonly quoted on many investment websites.

THE ESSENTIALS
* **Remember the objective** – every company wants to deliver a healthy return on equity.
* **Understand the process** – delivering return on equity is a three-stage process.
* **Check the gearing** – borrowing can increase return on equity, but can also expose a company to high interest commitments and/or reliance on the availability of third-party credit.
* **Check the asset turnover** – the more sales a company can drive from its assets, the higher the return on equity should be.
* **Check the profit margin** – the more cost efficient a company is, the higher will be its return on equity.
* **Construct a return on equity flowchart** – this explains how a company is combining gearing, asset turnover, and profit margin in order to produce a return on equity and can be used to identify its strengths and weaknesses.

* Check interest and dividends – interest cover provides an indication of a company's ability to meet interest payments, while dividend cover provides an indication of a company's ability to maintain dividend payments.

8

PRICE IS KING:

INVESTING IN SHARES 2

Many people are put off investing in shares because it all looks so complicated. In fact the principles of buying and selling shares are remarkably straightforward; it is no different to any other form of trading. If you trade in secondhand cars, that is an easy business to understand. You want to buy cars at one price and sell them at a higher price; hardly nuclear physics. Ironically, your ability to do this is all determined at the buy stage, at which point there are two disciplines you must adopt. First of all, you want to check the car over to make sure it is roadworthy. Secondly, you want to make sure that you are paying a fair price. If you fail in either of these tasks, you could well end up making a loss on the deal.

So it is when buying company shares. You want to make sure that the business is roadworthy (it is being well managed) and you want to ensure that you are paying a fair price for the shares. The previous chapter focused on the management issue. In this chapter our attention will be directed at the price issue.

This is a long chapter – the longest in the book – but I make no apologies for that. For most people it is shares that provide the most accessible opportunity to grow personal wealth significantly, so this form of investing deserves special attention.

Before proceeding any further, it is worth noting that companies can be divided into two broad categories:

* Privately owned companies.
* Publicly owned companies.

In a privately owned company, the shares are usually held by just a few people. The shares are not quoted on any form of stock exchange, so they can only be sold by private treaty. If you happen to own shares in a small family business and you decide to sell them, you have an immediate problem: you will have to shop around to find another individual who is prepared to buy them. Also, because they are not quoted on a stock exchange, there is no recognized price for the shares, so the price that is agreed will be down to the negotiating skills of the parties involved.

It is very common for companies to start life as privately owned but to become publicly owned as they grow and need access to more funds to finance their assets. An initial public offering (or IPO) refers to the process of getting a company's shares listed on a stock exchange. Various benefits open up when doing this:

* It provides access to millions of potential investors.
* It provides a market where investors can readily buy and sell the company's shares.
* It enables a market price to be established for the shares (no more private negotiations).

When people talk about investing in the stock market, they almost invariably mean buying and selling shares of companies listed on a recognized stock exchange and that is the focus of this chapter.

The first challenge: Who should make the decisions?

When investing in shares, there is a very important issue that needs to be addressed at the outset. Indeed, it is such an important issue that it really does demand attention before proceeding any further. Who should be making the investment decisions?

You can buy shares yourself or you can hire someone else to invest in shares on your behalf. In other words, you can adopt the doing it yourself (DIY) approach or the getting someone in (GSI) approach. Pursuing the latter option typically involves placing your money in a managed fund, where money from a variety of individuals is pooled and invested on their behalf. Three advantages of using managed funds are often cited:

* Expertise.
* Diversification.
* Economies of scale.

The typical sales patter of a managed fund will say that you can relax in the knowledge that your money is being handled by a professional fund manager. Also, because money is being pooled, the fund can be spread (diversified) over a far wider range of investments than you could hope to achieve as an individual, thereby reducing your risk. Finally, due to the size of the fund, transaction costs will be far lower than you could achieve personally.

Now it is time to look at the disadvantages of managed funds, of which there are also three:

* Overdiversification.
* Performance.
* Fees.

Starting with overdiversification, the more you diversify your investments, the more average your performance becomes. One of the arguments for using a professional fund manager is that they can spot investment opportunities that are going to benefit you. If they are spreading the fund over hundreds of companies, though, the impact of any such opportunities will be significantly diluted.

Moving on to the second issue, the evidence regarding performance is overwhelming. Over the years there have been numerous studies of fund performance, both academic and professional, and the conclusions are nearly always the same: most funds fail to beat the market in which they are investing. In fact, it is worse than that: studies show that most funds underperform the market. What this means is that, if a particular market has delivered returns of 10% over the past year, the majority of managed funds will deliver a return of less than 10%. The statistic that is often cited is that over 80% of managed funds underperform against the market in which they are investing. This statistic is based on the performance of funds over several years, which suggests that the true percentage is even higher: such studies exclude poorly performing funds that close down or have been absorbed into other funds in the meantime. So in reality we may well be looking at 90% or more of managed funds underperforming against the market, which is a frightening statistic.

If I am told that there is a less than 10% chance that if I place money with a fund manager they will be able to achieve even average returns, these are odds that I am not happy with at all. It is because of all these studies that you may hear apocryphal tales of monkeys with drawing pins randomly selecting companies from a newspaper and out-performing the supposed experts. The tragedy is that the research suggests that this could well be true.

Why do funds perform so badly? The most important contributing factor that is cited is nearly always the same: fees. When you place money with a managed fund you inevitably incur charges and it is these very charges that will damage your rate of return. Quite often, if you use the services of a financial adviser they will charge an upfront fee. This may be payable directly by you or be paid as a commission by the managed fund; either way, you will be footing the bill. Then there is an annual management fee charged by the fund manager. On top of this there are transaction fees. Every time the fund buys or sells shares it is paying a fee to do this and the more actively the fund is trading the higher these fees become. Then there are general administration costs that have to be paid (somebody has to pay for that coffee machine in the fund management office). Finally, depending on the fund, you may be charged an exit fee for having the gall to ask for your money back. Don't underestimate the impact of fees.

Suppose that you invest $100,000 in a share portfolio that is growing at 7% per annum. Being the shrewd investor you are, you understand the principle of compounding and have elected to reinvest all profits made along the way. If you opt to invest via a managed fund, we will assume that the annual total charges you incur will work out at a modest 2% of the fund value. The table overleaf compares what would happen to your fund if you invested the money directly on your own account and what would happen if you used the services of a fund manager.

YOU INVEST $100,000 IN A SHARE PORTFOLIO THAT IS GROWING AT 7% INTEREST PER ANNUM

	Total received back if invested directly	Total received back if fund manager used
After 5 years	$140,255	$126,779
After 10 years	$196,715	$160,730
After 20 years	$386,968	$258,343
After 30 years	$761,225	$415,236

THE IMPACT OF MANAGEMENT FEES

After five years, if you had invested your money directly, you would have made over $40,000 profit on your $100,000 investment. In reality it would be slightly lower than this, because you would have to pay trading fees when buying and selling shares, but the resulting figure should not be significantly lower than that. Using the services of a fund manager would have meant that you made less than $27,000. The longer you invest the money for, the more dramatic the impact of fees becomes. After 30 years you would be over $345,000 worse off if you opted to use the services of a fund manager instead of investing the money directly yourself – that is a lot of money to pay out for the convenience of letting someone else manage your investments for you.

There are two forces working against you when you use the services of a fund manager:

* Fees.
* Compounding.

If you invest the money yourself, you will be starting off with a $100,000 fund. If you pursue the managed fund route costing you 2% of the fund value each year, although you are handing over $100,000, only $98,000 will be invested; you are immediately $2,000 down and you have not even started investing yet. Incidentally, initial charges of 5% of the fund value or even more are not unheard of, so be warned. We are assuming an annual growth rate of 7%, so if you are investing the money directly, at the end of the first year your fund will have grown to $107,000, which you will be able to roll over into the second year.

By contrast, using a managed fund, it is your initial investment (after paying fees) of $98,000 that will grow by 7%, so you will be ending the year with $104,860. Bear in mind that the management charges are payable annually, so 2% of the fund value (which works out at $2,097) will be deducted as fees, leaving you with $102,763 as you enter the second year. Clearly, fees are eating away at your fund, but they are also having a more insidious effect. By reducing the value of the fund each year they are also reducing the annual profit you are earning on that fund, which can dramatically dilute the potential benefit of compounding.

One counter-argument to these figures is that an independent investor may not achieve the same returns as a fund manager, and that is what you are paying for. Given that it is commonly recognized that most funds underperform the market rate of return after fees, I do not think that is an argument worth pursuing any further. In fact, if you scan the internet you will find many studies indicating that there is no correlation between the payment of fees and performance.

I am afraid that there are no two ways about it: if you really want to grow your money in the stock market, you ought to do the investing yourself. Simply by taking control, you have already potentially improved your returns by refusing to pay fees. You can also benefit from the discipline that will help you ensure that you maximize your gains and minimize your losses if you adopt the 6R approach. Let's examine how this can be applied to shares.

Stage 1 – Recognize

Although the previous chapter was dedicated to assessing how effectively a company is being managed, according to the 6R approach that is not the first thing you should do when trying to identify potential investment opportunities. You have to find the company first before you can assess it. The first stage, then, is being able to recognize the opportunity: you need to find a company with potential.

When we looked at savings accounts and bonds, the first stage of the 6R approach was quite straightforward. All you had to do was find an account or bond that seemed to meet your investment requirements and then you could move straight on to the second stage and examine the rate of return on offer. A fundamental issue when dealing in shares is that you do not know what the rate of return is going to be. Indeed, identifying what the potential rate of return may be is the most intricate stage when assessing any share. Consequently, to avoid having to spend hours and hours trying to identify potential rates of return, you need some means of vetting shares at the outset. There are thousands of companies vying for investors' money. What is needed is a means of reducing this vast selection to maybe half a dozen (or even fewer) that may be of interest, and that is the challenge during the "Recognize" stage.

Before looking at individual companies, it is useful at the outset to develop a feel for what is happening to share prices overall. This demands an understanding of financial indices. Rather than telling you what has happened to the share price of an individual company, a **financial index** tells you what is happening to the share prices of a collection of companies.

One of the most famous of these indices is the Dow Jones Industrial Average (commonly abbreviated to just Dow Jones), which comments on the average share price movements of 30 of the largest publicly owned companies in the US. Closely aligned to this is the Standard and Poor's 500, which tracks the share performance of 500 of the most popular publicly owned companies traded in the US. Other indices you may encounter include the FTSE 100 (the 100 largest companies quoted on the London Stock Exchange), the Dax (the 30 major companies quoted on the Frankfurt Stock Exchange), the Nikkei (representing a spread of the top 225 companies quoted on the Tokyo Stock Exchange), and the Hang Seng (50 or so of the largest companies quoted on the Hong Kong Stock Exchange). This list is by no means exhaustive and you will find indices quoted on every major stock exchange around the world.

So what does an index tell us? Ironically, the actual numerical value of the index is of no concern. When the Dow Jones Industrial Average was first set up with just 12 companies in 1896, it stood at approximately 41. Of course, your typical shareholder has no interest in what has happened to US share prices since 1896! What is far more relevant is what has happened recently and in this respect it is the proportionate move that counts. Suppose an index was at 1,000 a year ago and now it is at 1,050, which is an increase of 5%. This tells us that the share prices of the companies incorporated within that index have increased on average by 5% in the last 12 months. If the index increased to 1,100, share prices would have increased by 10%, and so forth.

It is worth noting that most stock market indices only tell you what is happening to share prices; they do not as a general rule comment on dividends. So if an index increases by 10% during the year, although share prices have increased by this amount, the total return to share-holders after adding on dividends could be considerably higher.

As the companies represented within a major index typically account for a significant proportion of the total shares being traded on a specific stock exchange, changes in these indices are often used as an indicator of inves-tor confidence in the economy generally. An increasing index indicates an upward move in share prices, suggest-ing increasing investor confidence, while a decreasing index indicates a downward move in share prices, suggest-ing decreasing investor confidence. Looking at an index can therefore provide you with a feel for the mood of the market.

Having established what is happening to share prices generally, attention can now be turned to individual com-panies. It is not uncommon for many would-be investors to dive straight in and start looking at the figures. This is a big error. When it comes to considering any company as a potential investment, the first issue you ought to address is the product or service on offer – so step back and look at the business. After all, it is the product or service that gen-erates sales and without sales there will not be any profit.

There is a very important adage often quoted in the world of investing: "Don't invest in something that you don't understand." It is a simple rule: if you don't understand how the company makes money, don't part with your cash. So how do you feel about the business? Do you think it has a long-term future? Is it trading in a market that is expanding or contracting? Is there much competition? Could competition increase in the future? Only if you like the business idea should you then proceed to look at the numbers.

When it comes to numbers, share price data is readily available in the national press and on a variety of websites. It is a sad fact that many people avoid investing in shares because there seem to be so many figures to digest. Whether it is daily share price data or corporate trading results, it is all figures; they seem to be everywhere. For many people this is not a comfortable place to be (they probably still have nightmares about their math lessons at school), but don't let that put you off. When it comes to assessing share performance the figures are there to help you, not hinder you.

QUICK CHALLENGE
What do you think is the first figure a shareholder wants to see when a company announces its trading results?

Most people would assume that it is all about profit: provided that profits are increasing each year, shareholders will be happy. This is definitely not the case. A well-informed investor doesn't care if a company makes $1 million profit, $10 million profit, or even $100 million profit. What an investor should be preoccupied with is how much money the company is making specifically for them as an individual, which is not the same thing. Rather than focusing on the total profit a company has made, a far more useful figure for a shareholder is **earnings per share** (often abbreviated to EPS). This is key to understanding share prices and how they behave. Let's look at how it is worked out and then we can establish why it is such an important figure.

KEY MEASURE

$$\text{Earnings per share} = \frac{\text{Net income}}{\text{Number of shares}}$$

The earnings per share calculation starts with net income (also sometimes called profit after tax). This is the profit made after paying all the day-to-day costs of the business and all taxes due to the government. This figure is then divided by the number of shares in the company. If a company makes $10 million net income and there are 5 million shares in issue, earnings per share will be as follows:

$$\text{Earnings per share} = \frac{\text{Net income of \$10 million}}{\text{5 million shares}}$$

$$= \quad \$2$$

This says that on every share you own, the company has made you $2 profit. That is a far more useful figure than simply being told that the company has made $10 million profit during the last 12 months.

What can shareholders do with this profit? They have two options: they can withdraw it in the form of dividends, or they can reinvest it back into the business in the hope of achieving more profit in future years. It is like having a savings account. When you earn interest you have a choice:

you can take it out, or you might be tempted to leave the interest in the account to enable you to earn more interest next year. The really important point to note is that earnings per share tells you how much profit the company has made on each share before paying any dividend.

Now comes the critical question: Why is earnings per share more important than the profit figure? The problem is that when a company declares its profits have increased, it does not necessarily follow that the shareholders will be better off, because the company may have issued more shares. Suppose that a company needs to raise more money to finance future growth. In order to facilitate this, it has had to issue more shares. In fact, it has ended up doubling the number of shares in the business. If its profit goes up by 50%, the shareholders will be worse off, because their earnings per share will have decreased.

We have already established that when you buy a share in a company, what you are actually buying is a slice of its future profits. We can now be more precise. What you are actually buying is the future profit attributable to that specific share. In other words, you are buying future earnings per share – that is what drives share prices.

If you anticipate high earnings per share in the future, you will be willing to pay a high price for those shares now. If you anticipate low earnings per share in the future, you will only be willing to pay a low price for those shares. When share prices move, it suggests that expectations regarding future earnings per share are altering.

This begs a question: Who sets the share price? It is determined by supply and demand on the day. If lots of people want to buy shares in a company (on the assumption that they believe it will do well in the future) and very few people want to sell, the price of the share will start to

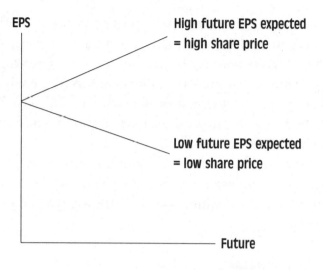

EARNINGS PER SHARE DRIVES SHARE PRICES

increase to entice sellers into the market. Conversely, if lots of people want to sell shares (because they are pessimistic about trading prospects) and very few people want to buy them, the price of the share will start to fall to entice buyers into the market. It is at this stage that the principles of share dealing become a little more involved. Pay particular attention to what I am about to say – it is critical to success in share investing.

What drives share prices is not how companies do in the future. Share prices are driven by how people *think* companies will do in the future, which is definitely not the same thing. If investors adopt the view that a company is going to make lots of money in the future (even if they are wrong in this assumption), the share price will be high. If they believe that the company is going to do badly (it is irrelevant whether they are right or wrong), the share price will be low.

The point to note from this discussion is that investors can be (and often are) wrong. This may be perceived as a problem, but it can also open up opportunities. If other investors are failing to notice the potential for a particular company when you do, buying shares now could make you a significant profit when other investors ultimately do realize the profit potential of the business and push the share price up. Fortunes can be made exploiting this principle, but losses can occur too.

It is time for some more jargon. Because share prices are driven by expectations, there are two basic approaches to share selection, which means there are two types of investors:

* Value investors.
* Growth investors.

Value investors are looking for companies that are out of favor, but those that they believe will recover or emerge in the not too distant future (these are sometimes called recovery or emerging stocks); they believe that the market is currently failing to realize the potential of these companies. **Growth investors** take the opposite stance: they are looking for companies that are already displaying strong profit growth and are already in favor, in the hope that they will continue to grow and become the powerhouses of the future. The approach you decide to adopt will ultimately affect the companies that you will find attractive, although there is nothing to stop you adopting a combination of the two approaches.

A good deal of information about how share prices are performing is readily available in the financial press and on financial websites. Let's have a look at the sort of information you might encounter for a single company and see what we can glean from it.

Name	Price	Change	52 week High	Low	Yield	P/E
	$	$	$	$	%	
Lisa Vann	19.72	+0.32	19.94	13.83	2.9	18.9

TYPICAL REPORTED DETAILS FOR A COMPANY'S SHARES

Normally the first figure people look at is the share price. This is fine if you already have shares in this company, because obviously you want to know if the value of your investment is going up or down. However, if you are trying to decide whether or not to buy these shares in the first place, the share price tells you nothing. Indeed, if you know someone who claims they dabble in shares, ask them what is the first figure they look at. If they say it is the share price, it's pretty obvious they haven't got a clue what they're talking about – and I will prove it. In this example we are looking at Lisa Vann with a share price of $19.72. Suppose you hear about another company called Hiram O'Terr, which has a share price of $138.04. Does it follow that Hiram O'Terr is seven times more successful than Lisa Vann? Of course not; but this begs a question: Why is its share price seven times higher?

A key driver of share prices is the number of shares in issue. A question I am often asked is: How do companies decide how many shares to issue? Suppose a company needs to raise $100 million to finance assets. There are lots of ways of raising that amount. The company could issue 100 million shares at $1 each; 50 million shares at $2 each; 10 million shares at $10 each; and so the options continue. The number of shares really does not matter; what counts is the amount of money the company wants to raise. The one caveat is that the fewer the shares the higher the share price will be, and thus the fewer the potential investors. If the company only issues two shares, it will need to find individuals who are prepared to invest at least $50 million each, whereas if the company issues 10 million shares at $10 each, it will appeal to a far wider audience. As a consequence, many companies believe that investors would like to see share prices trading within certain limits, what is known as the tradable range.

If a share price is very low, investors may be tempted to regard the shares as cheap and feel that the company's prospects are poor. At the other extreme, if a share price is very high, investors might view it as expensive and therefore not representative of good value. In reality, a company with a share price of $1 may have equally good trading prospects (maybe even better) than those of a company with a share price of $500. It is all a matter of perception. There is no formal definition of a low share price or a high share price, so what is deemed too low or too high will vary from one company to another. But how can a company manage its share price?

There are two markets within which shares can be traded:

∗   Primary market.
∗   Secondary market.

The **primary market** is concerned with the issue of brand new shares, whereas the **secondary market** is concerned with the trading of secondhand shares.

Suppose a company is about to offer shares for the first time on a stock exchange and you decide to subscribe for some – the company gets your money, in return for which you receive shares. You have just traded in the primary market. A couple of years pass and you decide you now want to sell the shares. But who can you sell them to? You can't go back to the company and ask for your money back, as it is all tied up in assets. If you want to liquidate your investment, you have no option but to sell your shares to other investors – you are about to enter the secondary market.

When releasing shares in the primary market, companies can control the price, because it is up to them how many shares are to be issued. But how can they control the price once their shares are being traded in the secondary market? Well, they have a couple of party tricks up their sleeve.

If a company feels that its share price is getting too low, it can undergo what is called a **share consolidation**. This involves going to all the existing shareholders and replacing their existing shareholdings with fewer shares. For example, if a company decides to do a one-for-two consolidation, it will replace every two shares currently in issue with one share. This will result in the share price doubling, which if you are a shareholder may seem like great news, but bear in mind that you now only have half as many shares, so you are no better off. What the company has managed to do, though, is raise its share price to a level that it deems will be more attractive to investors.

Going to the other extreme, if the share price is seen to be too high, it is argued that this can put investors off buying the shares – particularly private investors. In this situation a company can carry out a **share split**, the opposite of a share consolidation. This involves replacing existing shareholdings with an increased number of shares. In a two-for-one split, a company will increase the number of shares so that each shareholder winds up with two shares for every one owned previously. The share price will halve, but bear in mind that each shareholder now has twice as many shares. They are no worse off, but the company has managed to move its share price down to what it regards as a more attractive level. In the financial news you will regularly encounter stories about companies splitting and consolidating shares in order to maneuver their share price into a more attractive zone.

Although share splits and share consolidations are designed to encourage share dealing, they can also have a more subtle impact on the perceived value of the company. Investors are always looking for clues regarding future trading performance, so that when a company announces a split or a consolidation, they will be trying to work out why it has resorted to this tactic. Share splits can sometimes have a positive effect on share prices, as investors may view the tactic as a company announcing that it sees strong profit growth in the future and hence the need for the share split. Share consolidations can sometimes have the opposite effect, with investors assuming that a company is declaring it cannot trade its way up to a higher share price, hence the need for the share consolidation. All of this is based on perception and investors can be wrong, but always be aware that such a move could (in the short term at least) affect share performance.

So what have we learned by comparing Lisa Vann's share price with that of Hiram O'Terr? Well, maybe Hiram O'Terr has fewer shares, but we are not even certain about that, so we have learned absolutely nothing. This is evidence indeed that comparing share prices is a complete waste of time.

Something else the financial press usually tells us is by how much the share price has changed in the preceding

24-hour trading period. In the case of Lisa Vann, the share price has increased by 32 cents. Over time we would expect share prices of companies to increase as the value of the company itself grows. However, on a day-to-day basis the number of shares being offered for sale will rarely equal the number of shares that investors want to buy, so there will inevitably be daily fluctuations in the price. We would not expect these fluctuations to be dramatic, though, unless there has been a significant shift in investors' sentiment. This reinforces the view that when dealing in shares, think long term.

Although daily share price movements are of interest, movements over several months can provide a more useful indicator of how expectations regarding future performance are changing. To assist in this, it is common practice to have **52-week high** and **52-week low** figures reported. These tell us the highest price and the lowest price a share has reached in the preceding 52-week period. In the case of Lisa Vann, it has seen its share price go as high as $19.94 and as low as $13.83. How does this help us?

There is a rule of thumb that is often employed when looking at these figures, which runs as follows. If a company is close to its 52-week high and most of its peers are nowhere near their 52-week high, this would suggest that expectations regarding this specific business have recently improved. However, if a company is close to its 52-week low and most of its peers are nowhere near their 52-week low, this would suggest that expectations regarding this specific business have recently been downgraded.

Lisa Vann has a share price of $19.72, which is certainly close to its 52-week high of $19.94. If most of its peers are in the same situation, this would indicate that the market generally is picking up and there is nothing that would single this company out for individual attention. However, if most of its peers are nowhere near their 52-week high, this would suggest that something must have happened recently that has led investors to enhance their expectations of future performance in this particular organization.

Examining 52-week highs and 52-week lows is a useful practice to identify companies that may warrant further investigation. The only problem is that nobody has ever defined what is meant by the term "close to," so it is a useful rule of thumb, but there is still a great deal of subjectivity attached to it.

Another use for the 52-week figures is to assess a share's volatility. A wide gap between the high and low prices suggests high volatility, while a narrow gap suggests low volatility. The difference between these two figures is known as the **range**. In the case of Lisa Vann, the range is $6.11 (the difference between the 52-week high of $19.94 and the 52-week low of $13.83). Obviously, a $6.11 fluctuation is far more significant for a share that is trading at around $20 than one that is trading at $100. A simple way to put this into context is to look at the range relative to the share price. In the case of Lisa Vann, the 52-week range of $6.11 represents 31% of the current share price of $19.72. The bigger the percentage, the more volatile the share price has been.

All of the figures we have looked at so far relate to share prices and how they are moving. Another figure often quoted in relation to share price performance is yield, which is an abbreviation for **dividend yield**. This considers the most recent annual dividend per share as a percentage of the current share price.

KEY MEASURE

$$\text{Dividend yield} = \frac{\text{Annual dividend}}{\text{Share price}} \times 100\%$$

Lisa Vann is quoting a yield of 2.9%, which tells us that, based on the previous year's dividend and assuming dividends remain the same in the future, if you bought $100 worth of shares in the company today, you should expect to earn about $2.90 a year in the form of dividends. If you are looking for shares that generate a healthy income, this information will be particularly relevant to you. You can determine what is a low yield and what is a high yield by studying the yields of competitors; you will rapidly develop a feel for what is the norm.

Don't rush out and buy shares in a company simply because it has a high yield, though; bear in mind this percentage is based on last year's payout. The critical issue is whether or not the company will be able to continue paying out a dividend in the future. Looking at the dividend cover (introduced in the previous chapter) can be very useful in this respect, as it states how many times profit covers dividends.

GROW YOUR OWN MONEY
If you are investing in shares for income, always check the dividend yield and the dividend cover.

Some people argue that the problem with looking at yield is that it only comments on one way you can benefit from owning shares: through dividend income. As we know, you can also benefit if the value of the share increases, which yield tells you nothing about. However, there are investors that believe yield can also be useful when it comes to assessing the future trading prospects of a company. How can this be done?

When a company makes a profit, it can either be paid out to shareholders in the form of a dividend or reinvested back into the business so that it can make more profit in the future. If a company has limited growth prospects, it would not be logical for it to keep reinvesting money back into the business. As a result, companies that are fairly mature and/or have limited growth potential tend to be associated with increased levels of dividend. By contrast, if companies are expected to grow quickly in the future, they will need finance to achieve this. As a general principle, high-growth companies tend to be associated with low dividends or even no dividend payments at all.

On this basis, you might be tempted to think that low yields are indicative of a successful future, as they suggest lots of profit being reinvested to grow the business. Unfortunately, there are other reasons for companies having low yields – they may not be making any money in the first place or they may have a serious cash flow problem. Never make an investment decision based on yield alone. It is a useful figure but, in the case of low yields, more information is needed before you can make an informed assessment of what is going on.

One other figure is commonly quoted in relation to share performance and it is generally acknowledged to be the most useful of all of the statistics that are regularly reported. It is the **P/E ratio** (an abbreviation for the price/earnings ratio); also sometimes called the profit multiple or earnings multiple of a company. Although this is a very useful measure, it is also unfortunately a little technical, so you need to apply some logic to make sense of it.

We have already noted that the first figure a share-holder is interested in when reviewing the trading results of a company is earnings per share. The P/E ratio focuses on this figure and provides an indication of how investors believe it is going to perform in the future. It achieves this by taking the share price and dividing it by the earnings per share.

KEY MEASURE

$$P/E = \frac{\text{Share price}}{\text{Earnings per share}}$$

If a company has a share price of \$20 and the earnings per share last year was \$2, the P/E ratio will be 10 (\$20 divided by \$2). This tells us that at present, investors are prepared to pay 10 times the current earnings of a share to get their hands on it. In other words, they are prepared to pay 10 times profit. It follows that, if a company has a high P/E ratio, investors are paying far more than current profits to get their hands on a share. Why would they be prepared to do this? They must surely believe that earnings per share is going to grow fast in the future.

Conversely, if a company has a low P/E ratio, the opposite is true: investors are not paying much more than current profits to get their hands on a share, suggesting low expectations of future performance. In the case of Lisa Vann, investors are currently prepared to pay 18.9 times current profit.

At last, we have a measure that is comparable across companies. Unlike yield (which only examines the share price in relation to dividends paid), the P/E ratio looks at the share price in relation to total profits earned.

The important point to note about a P/E ratio is that it is commenting on future performance relative to current earnings. It does not tell you which companies are successful and which are not. A company might have a high P/E ratio simply because last year it made very little profit; after all, it is often far easier to grow a small profit figure than a large profit figure. As a result, high P/E ratios are often associated with younger companies that are expected to grow rapidly in the future. Lower P/E ratios tend to be associated with more mature businesses where the potential for aggressive profit growth is more limited.

The main reason the P/E ratio is so popular among investors is that it is commenting on the price. You may have heard people saying that a share is cheap or expensive, but what does this mean? If shares in Maxi Price Trading are $100 while shares in Mini Price Trading are $5, does this mean that shares in Maxi Price Trading are expensive while shares in Mini Price Trading are cheap? It is like buying a car. If you are told that someone is selling a car for $16,000, is that cheap or expensive? To answer this you need to look at the car. Similarly, to assess a share price, you need to look at the company. Bear in mind the main benefit of owning shares is that it entitles you to a share of that company's profits. By linking these profits to the share price, the P/E ratio is not only commenting on perceived profit growth, it is also providing an indication of how expensive the shares are.

If a company has a high P/E ratio, you are paying a high price relative to current profits. If a company has a low P/E ratio, you are paying a low price relative to current profits. It is at this stage that the difference between value and growth investing becomes evident. Value investors, which include some of the world's most successful investors, are looking for bargains and will be attracted to companies with low P/E ratios. Growth investors are quite happy to consider companies with far higher P/E ratios because they are looking for companies that already demonstrate solid performance and have the potential to grow still further.

Based on performance over the past few years, coupled with the advent of a more globalized economy, the following table provides a rough rule of thumb for interpreting P/E ratios. Bear in mind that if a company is loss making, it cannot have a P/E ratio because there is no profit figure.

VALUE	INTERPRETATION
No P/E	Absence of a P/E ratio normally indicates a company that is currently loss making
Less than 10	Low earnings growth anticipated
10 to 20	Reasonable earnings growth anticipated
More than 20	High earnings growth anticipated

INTERPRETING THE P/E RATIO

These are very broad-brush assessments and there will be exceptions. For example, if a company's profit falls temporarily, the P/E ratio will increase. Also a company's perceived risk can lead to variations in the price investors are prepared to pay for its shares. Generally, the higher the risk attached to a company, the lower will be its share price, resulting in a lower P/E ratio. The most effective way to assess a company's P/E ratio is to compare it against some of its peers.

There is one situation that demands special attention. When a P/E is zero there is no profit figure, so it is meaningless to talk about how many times the share price exceeds the profit figure. Be aware that in this unique circumstance the P/E ratio is unable to comment on the share price.

We have now reviewed the key figures commonly reported in the financial press and on investment websites. The table below summarizes what can be gleaned from them.

KEY FIGURE	VALUE	CONCLUSION
Share price	Close to 52-week high	If peers are nowhere near their 52-week high, this suggests breaking news that is upgrading future trading prospects.
	Close to 52-week low	If peers are nowhere near their 52-week low, this suggests breaking news that is downgrading future trading prospects.
52-week high/low	Wide range	The share price is volatile.
	Narrow range	The share price is reasonably stable.
Yield	High	Large dividends are being paid out, suggesting limited growth opportunities.
	Low	Low dividends are being paid out, suggesting EITHER profits being reinvested to exploit future growth opportunities OR the company is experiencing financial difficulties and is unable to pay healthy dividends.
P/E	High	Strong growth in earnings per share is anticipated.

	Low	Poor earnings per share performance is anticipated, while a zero value usually indicates a business that is currently loss making.

ASSESSING SHARE PRICE PERFORMANCE

I must emphasize that this table provides general guidelines only and you will encounter variations from time to time. Nevertheless, for the majority of cases it should help give you a sense of where a company may be in terms of its trading capabilities.

Given the huge array of companies available on most stock exchanges, I personally find that a fast way of identifying potential investment opportunities is to restrict my attention primarily to the P/E ratio and dividend yield figures. The following matrix details the various combinations encountered.

P/E ratio	High P/E + Low yield High-growth company	High P/E + High yield Powerhouse
	Low P/E + Low yield Tough trading	Low P/E + High yield Mature company

Dividend yield

P/E RATIO AND YIELD COMBINATIONS

When talking about low and high values here, interpret this
as either being below or above the average market value.
This does not mean that you have to work out the average
P/E ratio or yield figure, though. Just a quick glance over a
selection of companies currently being quoted on a stock
exchange will enable you to readily identify an approximate average value for each measure. Having done this,
you can then determine whether any yield or P/E figure
should be classed as low or high.

Let's look at how to interpret each of the possible
P/E ratio and yield combinations. I must emphasize that
these are broad-brush interpretations (there will always be
exceptions), but they should cover the majority of situations you are likely to encounter in practice.

COMBINATION	INTERPRETATION
High P/E + High yield	A high P/E ratio is indicative of a business that is expected to deliver strong earnings growth in the future. Combine this with robust income, as indicated by a high yield figure, and you have found a veritable powerhouse. Not surprisingly, growth investors who want a reliable income stream will find this sort of company particularly attractive.
High P/E + Low yield	A high P/E ratio coupled with a low yield is indicative of a business that is reinvesting most of its profits (hence the low yield) in anticipation of strong earnings growth in the future. Once again, this will prove attractive to growth investors, but here the attraction is primarily the capital gain.

COMBINATION	INTERPRETATION
Low P/E + High yield	Companies with fairly modest P/E ratios but strong yields tend to be more mature businesses. Given limited growth opportunities, they favor paying dividends out to shareholders. These sorts of companies tend to attract investors who are more concerned with generating a reliable income stream.
Low P/E + Low yield	Low P/E ratios coupled with low yields are typically indicative of fledgling businesses, or businesses that are finding trading tough and may even be experiencing cash flow issues. This is the domain of value investors. These companies are currently out of favor and therefore priced cheaply. Value investors are looking for companies like these that they expect will be able to turn their fortunes around in the future, thereby providing opportunities for significant capital gains.

INTERPRETING P/E RATIO AND YIELD COMBINATIONS

As you can see, once you have decided what your objectives are as an investor, scanning the P/E ratios and associated yields provides a time-effective means of working through share data in order to identify those companies that may prove to be of interest.

GROW YOUR OWN MONEY
Scanning companies' P/E ratios and yields provides a quick method of identifying potential investment opportunities.

Stage 2 – Reward

Having identified a company that is of interest, you now need to establish whether or not it is capable of delivering a healthy rate of return in the future. This involves looking at the company in a little more depth, the intention being to satisfy yourself on two points:

* The business is being well managed and is capable of delivering healthy profits in the future.
* The current share price represents a fair valuation of the company's profit potential.

This is by far the most intricate stage of the 6R approach when it comes to investing in shares. It is at this stage that the "four-figure trick" introduced in the previous chapter comes into play. Obtain the annual reports for the last two years for the company under consideration. The easiest way to do this is to visit the corporate website and go to the "Investor Relations" section, where there is usually a facility to download the reports free of charge. You can then calculate the following figures for each of the last two years:

* Gearing.
* Asset turnover.
* Profit margin.
* Return on equity.

These can then be integrated into a return on equity flowchart, which will explain any changes in return on equity performance, while at the same time highlighting the company's strengths and/or weaknesses. Also look at its interest cover and dividend cover. Carrying out this analysis, which only takes a few minutes to do, enables you to assess whether or not the business is indeed being well managed.

GROW YOUR OWN MONEY
To assess how well a company is being managed, construct a return on equity flowchart.

If you are satisfied with how the business is being run and are confident that it will continue to be well managed in the future, you can turn your attention to the issue of pricing. Although we have a measure that enables us to assess in overall terms how well a business is being managed – return on equity – what we do not have yet is a measure that enables us to assess the share price. The P/E ratio gives an indication of what is expected to happen to earnings growth in the future and provides a feel for whether the shares appear cheap or expensive. What it does not do, however, is give an indication of whether or not the share price represents good value. Don't confuse cost with value for money. Although Lamborghini has a reputation for building expensive cars, the high price tag could still be perceived as representing good value given the quality of vehicle being acquired. Shares are no different.

To determine whether or not a share price represents good value for money, we are going to have to build a link between the company's reported results (given in the annual report) and the share price. As a first step, let's revisit the financial statements of Spotter Gooden, introduced in the previous chapter.

SPOTTER GOODEN FINANCIAL STATEMENTS

Balance sheet ($m)

Assets	50
Liabilities	−30
Shareholders' funds	20

Income statement ($m)

Sales	80
Costs	−76
Net income	4

You may recall that, according to the balance sheet, if this company sold off all its assets for $50 million and paid off all its liabilities of $30 million, the shareholders would walk away with $20 million. This is the book value of the business; in theory at least, it is the value of the business if it ceased trading tomorrow.

Identifying the book value of a company is a useful exercise as it forms the basis of a measure that can be particularly beneficial when it comes to assessing share prices. The **book value per share** is established by dividing the company's book value by the number of shares in issue.

KEY MEASURE

$$\text{Book value per share} = \frac{\text{Shareholders' funds}}{\text{Number of shares}}$$

In order to perform this calculation, you need to know the number of shares that have been issued. This demands that you delve into the annual report a little deeper. You need to go to the section called "Notes to the Accounts" or a similar equally exciting title. Within these notes you will be told the number of shares the company has issued.

Suppose there are 4 million shares in Spotter Gooden. In this instance, the book value of each share will be $5 ($20 million worth of shareholders' funds divided by 4 million shares). This tells us that, in theory at least, for every share in issue there is $5 physically tied up in the company. In normal circumstances the share price of the company would not be expected ever to drop below this value, but if it did, this could suggest serious problems ahead. So even at this early stage, we are already beginning to develop share price expectations for this particular business.

Before going any further, it is important to appreciate that there are two different methods available for valuing a business:

* Book value.
* Market value.

We already know what the term book value means. The **market value** (or market capitalization) is worked out by multiplying the share price by the number of shares in issue. Typically the market value would be expected to exceed the book value and the difference between the two valuations is known as **goodwill**. So what is goodwill?

The book value refers to the assets of the business (less any liabilities). This is the price that investors would be prepared to pay to get their hands on the company's assets such as properties, inventory, equipment, and vehicles. Why would investors be prepared to pay more than this? People dress up goodwill: they say it is the brand; it is the customer base; it is the management expertise. These

all affect the value of goodwill, but goodwill itself is something very specific: it is the purchase price of future profits.
When you buy a company, you are not just acquiring its
assets, you are also acquiring a profit stream. If you believe
that future profits are going to be buoyant, you will pay a
high price to get your hands on them. Conversely, if you
believe future that profits are going to be virtually non-
existent, you will pay a very low price.

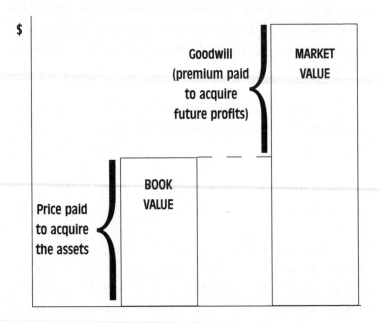

TWO WAYS TO VALUE A COMPANY

We can now be more scientific when it comes to placing
a value on a company's shares. To determine whether or
not a share price offers good value for money, what you
need to do is determine whether or not the valuation of
the goodwill is realistic. This introduces the measure we
have been looking for – the measure that enables us to

assess share prices. It is called the **market to book ratio** (also known as the price to book or P/B ratio). There are two ways it can be worked out, but both approaches provide the same answer. You can look at the market value of the company relative to its book value, or you can take the share price relative to the book value per share. The latter method tends to be the one most commonly adopted in practice and that is the one we are going to use here.

KEY MEASURE

$$\text{Market to book ratio} = \frac{\text{Share price}}{\text{Book value per share}}$$

To make sense of what this measure is saying, we need to understand a little more about the dynamics of how share prices are set. In reality, you will never have to go through the various steps we are about to cover here, but only by understanding where share prices come from can you ever hope to be in a position to assess whether you feel a share is overvalued or undervalued, so this will be time well invested.

To keep things as simple as possible, we are going to confine our attention to profit over the next year. In practice, this would be done by considering profit performance over several years. Notwithstanding this, the principle remains the same. When you buy shares in a company, either consciously or subconsciously you are taking a position on its future profitability.

Suppose your best guess is that over the next year Spotter Gooden will once again make $4 million profit. According to the balance sheet, shareholders currently have $20 million physically invested in the business. This means that the company is expected to deliver a 20% return on equity ($4 million profit as a percentage of $20 million worth of shareholders' funds). However, it is not the total profit figure that drives share prices; it is earnings per share. The higher the anticipated future earnings per share of a company, the higher will be its share price. Given that Spotter Gooden has 4 million shares, an annual profit of $4 million will provide an earnings per share of $1 and it is this figure that is going to determine the share price.

QUICK CHALLENGE

You are being offered a share that will make you a profit of $1 each year. What is the maximum price you would be prepared to pay for it?

To answer this, you have to decide what rate of return you are looking for. Suppose you are looking for a minimum annual return of 10% on shares; if you can achieve this, you will be happy. Using this expectation as the guideline, we are going to establish how much you would be prepared to pay for shares in Spotter Gooden.

If you were offered shares in Spotter Gooden for $2 you would no doubt snap them up, because you would be making a $1 annual profit on a $2 investment; that is a 50% rate of return, which is very handsome indeed. If you paid $4 per share, the $1 profit would provide you with a 25% rate of return, which is still significantly above what you are looking for. In fact, the highest price you would be prepared to bid in this scenario would be $10. At that price, $1 profit would provide you with your minimum acceptable rate of return of 10%. You would not even be willing to pay $10.01 because, at that price, $1 profit represents less than 10% of your investment. On this basis, if most investors are looking for a similar rate of return, the market price of the share would be set at $10.

Look at what we have just done. We started with a profit forecast for a company and we have now worked out what the share price should be. We can now return to the market to book ratio.

We have already noted that the book value per share for Spotter Gooden is $5. We have also just worked out that, if investors anticipate the company will deliver a 20% return on equity in the future and are looking for a minimum rate of return on their investment of 10%, the market price for the company's shares would be $10. The market to book ratio can now be established:

$$\text{Market to book ratio} = \frac{\text{Share price of \$10}}{\text{Book value per share of \$5}}$$

$$= 2$$

The market price of the share will be double the book value.

Let's work through three more scenarios. This might seem a bit involved, but it is worth persevering with, because if you can get your head round this you are really beginning to understand how the share market works. Don't get too preoccupied with the figures – all you need to understand is the logic.

Suppose Spotter Gooden is expected to deliver a profit of $3 million over the next year, which represents a return on equity of 15% on the $20 million physically invested within the business. Given that 4 million shares are in issue, the earnings per share works out at 75 cents. In this circumstance, to achieve a 10% return on your investment, the maximum you would now be prepared to pay for each share would be $7.50. The market to book ratio will therefore be 1.5 (the market price of $7.50 divided by the book value of $5) – the market price of the share will be one and a half times its book value.

If the company is expected to deliver a profit of $2 million over the next year, this represents a return on equity of 10% on the $20 million physically invested within the business. Dividing this profit figure by 4 million shares gives an earnings per share of 50 cents. In this circumstance, to achieve a 10% return on your investment, the maximum you would now be prepared to pay for each share would be $5. The market to book ratio would be 1 – the market price of the share would equate to its book value.

Finally, if the company is expected to deliver a profit of $1 million over the next year, this represents a return on equity of 5% on the $20 million physically invested within the business. Given that 4 million shares are in issue, the earnings per share would become 25 cents. In this circumstance, to achieve a 10% return on your investment, the maximum you would be prepared to pay for each share would be $2.50, giving a market to book ratio of 0.5 (the market price of $2.50 divided by the book value of $5). The market price of the share will be half of its book value.

Let's summarize the four scenarios we have just worked through.

FORECASTED PROFIT	FORECASTED RETURN ON EQUITY	FORECASTED EPS	SHARE PRICE	MARKET TO BOOK
$1,000,000	5%	$0.25	$2.50	0.5
$2,000,000	10%	$0.50	$5.00	1.0
$3,000,000	15%	$0.75	$7.50	1.5
$4,000,000	20%	$1.00	$10.00	2.0

THE LINK BETWEEN FORECASTED PROFITS AND SHARE PRICES

This is probably the toughest piece of logic you are going to need to tackle throughout the book. It is true that the link between forecasted company profits and share values is a little involved and it does demand some concentration on your part but, as mentioned previously, once you understand the logic you can be far more objective when looking at share prices in the future.

When the market to book ratio is 1, the company is expected to deliver a return on equity of 10% in the future. We have also noted that 10% is the minimum rate of return that you (and other shareholders) would accept. This is the market rate of return: the rate of return the market is looking for. It follows that when the market to book ratio is 1, the company is expected in the future to generate the minimum acceptable rate of return. In a scenario where the market to book ratio is 0.5, the company is still expected to generate a profit in the future, but the return on equity of 5% is half the minimum rate the market would normally accept. By contrast, when the market to book ratio is 2, the anticipated return on equity of 20% is double what the market would normally expect. Consolidating these results places you in a position where you can make sense of what a market to book ratio is telling you.

MARKET TO BOOK RATIO	INTERPRETATION
Less than 1	The company is expected to generate a return from shareholders' funds that is less than the market rate, implying inefficient use of funds.
1	The company is expected to generate the market rate of return from shareholders' funds.
More than 1	The company is expected to generate a return from shareholders' funds that is in excess of the market rate, implying efficient use of funds.

INTERPRETING THE MARKET TO BOOK RATIO

The market to book ratio can be seen to be commenting on how effectively a company is expected to manage shareholders' funds in the future: the more effectively this can be done, the higher the ratio will be. The real power of this statistic, though, and the reason we are dedicating quite a lot of time to understanding it, is that it provides a fast means of assessing whether a share price is overvalued, undervalued, or just about right.

Professional financial analysts use a wide variety of techniques to assess share prices, many of them involving complex financial models, yet it is very rare to find two analysts who agree with each other; indeed, it is not unusual to find one analyst who believes that a share is going to crash over the next 12 months and another who believes that the same share is going to soar. It all comes down to what has been said previously: nobody knows for sure what the future holds.

What I am about to walk you through is the basic approach that I adopt when assessing share prices. We have already established that there is a relationship between the market to book ratio and anticipated future return on equity. For example, we would expect the market to book ratio to be 2 when a company is expected to deliver a return on equity in the future that is double the market rate of return. It follows that we would expect the market to book ratio to be 3 when a company is expected to deliver a return on equity in the future that is treble the market rate of return, and so on. It is this relationship that we are going to use to assess share prices.

Suppose you expect a company in the future to deliver a return on equity that is double the market rate. In this situation, you would expect the market to book ratio to be close to 2. If the current market to book ratio is significantly below 2, this is indicative of a share that may be undervalued. The share price reflects a return on equity below that of which you believe the company is capable, providing potential for a capital gain when the company is seen to outperform expectations. If the current market to book ratio is well above 2, this is indicative of a share that may be overvalued. The share price reflects a return on equity that is above what you believe the company can deliver, suggesting that the share price may fall when the company fails to meet expectations.

It follows that all we need to assess a share price are two pieces of information:

∗ Market to book ratio.
∗ Forecasted return on equity.

We know how to work out the market to book ratio. This may not even be necessary in most circumstances, as the market to book ratio is a figure that can be found on many investment websites.

The only tricky figure to identify is the forecasted return on equity. Bear in mind that nobody knows what this figure is actually going to be, so all we can rely on is some educated guesswork. A good starting point is to consult the company's return on equity flowchart and study performance over the past couple of years:

∗ What return on equity has the company been
   delivering in the past?
∗ Year on year, is the return on equity increasing or
   decreasing?
∗ Is there any news that suggests whether future
   performance is expected to improve or deteriorate?
∗ If you're happy to do some research, what returns
   on equity are other companies in the same sector
   achieving?

Answering these questions should provide you with a rough feel for what you believe would be a realistic return on equity for the company to achieve in the future.

You find a company that appears to be well managed. The market to book ratio is 1.5. Return on equity during the last year was 21% and 17% in the previous year. Recent news articles suggest that the prospects for the sector generally are improving. On this basis, you believe that a future return on equity of 25% is realistic. All we now need to do is to determine what, if your forecasts turn out to be right, the market to book ratio for this company ought to be. To do this we need to know what the market rate of return is. Many studies have been carried out to try to identify this figure with, not surprisingly, a vast array of conclusions. I like to keep things simple. We noted in the previous chapter that most companies want to achieve a minimum return on equity of 10%. If we adopt this as an approximation for a reasonable market rate of return, we can readily identify what an appropriate market to book ratio should be for any forecasted return on equity figure.

If the market rate of return is 10%:

∗   A forecasted return on equity of 5% would be half the market rate, resulting in a forecasted market to book ratio of 0.5.
∗   A forecasted return on equity of 10% would be equivalent to the market rate, resulting in a forecasted market to book ratio of 1.
∗   A forecasted return on equity of 20% would be double the market rate, resulting in a forecasted market to book ratio of 2.
∗   A forecasted return on equity of 30% would be treble the market rate, resulting in a forecasted market to book ratio of 3.

And so on. Although here we are assuming a market rate of return of 10%, you can substitute any figure you choose, whatever you believe would be the minimum rate of return that most investors would accept on the stock exchange you are intending to trade on.

Now we can return to the company that has caught your eye. You're expecting it to produce a future return on equity of 25%, which, assuming a market rate of return of 10%, should result in a market to book ratio of 2.5 (the forecasted rate of return is 2.5 times the market rate). However, the current market to book ratio is only 1.5, suggesting that you may have identified a share that is currently undervalued, so you may well be looking at an attractive investment opportunity.

GROW YOUR OWN MONEY
Comparing a forecasted market to book ratio against the current market to book ratio provides a fast means of assessing a share price.

When examining return on equity for a company, and the associated market to book ratio, be aware that these can vary significant from one industry to another. As a general rule, industries that are asset intensive (e.g., manufacturing) tend to produce returns on equity that are significantly below those produced by sectors that require few assets (e.g., management consultancy). Borrowing also has an impact. We established in the previous chapter that high-geared companies are capable of delivering a far higher return on equity than their low-geared counterparts.

Now, I expect some professional investment managers to express horror at this approach, claiming that the value of a share is "the discounted value of all future cash flows." Most directors I have worked with confess that forecasting cash flows for their own business, over just the next few months, is often fraught with difficulties. So I am at a loss at how a financial analyst, sitting in an office staring at a spreadsheet, can claim to be able to forecast cash flows for companies over the next few years with any degree of accuracy. All I can say is that this approach to assessing share prices has stood me in good stead time and time again.

The one caveat to bear in mind when applying the above approach is that any conclusions drawn are based on an estimated market rate of return and an estimated future return on equity – and estimates can be wrong. This approach therefore cannot guarantee that you have found shares that are undervalued or overvalued. What it does do, though, is give you a sense of whether a share *may* be currently overvalued or undervalued, and that is valuable information for any investor. Understanding a little about general market behavior can greatly help in this respect.

The first point to note is that, bizarre as it sounds, if the general market is accurate in its forecasts, the price you pay for the share becomes irrelevant.

Returning to the table linking share prices to forecasted profits, you will see that if the company is expected to produce a 5% return on equity, the earnings per share will be 25 cents and the price you will pay for the share will be $2.50. In that situation, you will get a 10% return on your investment (a 25 cents return as a percentage of your $2.50 investment). If by contrast the company is expected to produce a 20% return on equity, the earnings per share will be $1 and the price you will now pay for the share will be $10. Ironically, you will still achieve a 10% return on your investment (a $1 return as a percentage of your $10 investment).

This is an illustration of a principle called the efficient market hypothesis, which says that if the market is always right, you may as well simply stick a pin in a list of companies to pick your investments. In other words, this principle suggests that the overall rate of return you will achieve as a shareholder will be the same regardless of the companies you select, because variations in corporate performance will already have been factored into the share prices. It's a nice theory, but many investors disagree with it.

The truth is that nobody knows for certain what is going to happen tomorrow, yet alone in the next few years. Even if you present two people with exactly the same information, their interpretations can differ markedly. Suppose the outside air temperature is 20 °C. Is that hot or cold? Some people will argue that is quite warm and others will say that is quite cool. There is no disputing the temperature – it is 20 °C – but whether it is hot or cold is a matter of interpretation. So it is in the corporate world: you can present two investors with the same information about a company and get wildly differing views of its trading prospects.

I was once involved with the flotation of a major business on the London Stock Exchange. Two investment banks had been called in to assess its market value so that a launch price for the shares could be determined. Obviously, both banks had full access to the trading results of the business and the insights of the management team. After 18 months the two banks (which both, incidentally, charged millions of dollars for their services) agreed that this particular business was definitely worth somewhere between $7 billion and $12 billion. That is a little like having your house valued and being informed that it is worth somewhere between half a million and a million dollars. Forecasting the future is a remarkably inaccurate science, but it is the very fact that it can be so wildly inaccurate that provides opportunities to improve returns.

Let's continue our investigation of the table that links forecasted profits and share prices. We have established that, if you were expecting the company to deliver a 5% return on equity in the future, the share price would be set at $2.50. Now suppose the management team reveal a strategy whereby they believe they can increase return on equity by a full 5 percentage points, to 10%. Based on the figures in the table, if a return on equity of 10% is now anticipated, the share price would increase to $5 – it would double.

Contrast this with the situation where you are already expecting the company to deliver a 15% return on equity in the future. In this situation the share price would be $7.50. Now suppose the management team presents a strategy to increase that rate of return by a full 5 percentage points, to 20%. If investors genuinely believed that a return on equity of 20% would now be delivered, the share price would increase to $10. In this second scenario the share price would increase by a third, from $7.50 to $10.

These two scenarios highlight some very important principles of which you need to be aware when it comes to buying and selling shares.

The first point to note is that it is changes in expectations that drive share price performance – how well the company is doing is irrelevant. If expectations of future trading performance are revised upward, the share price will increase. That is logical: improving performance results in an increasing share price. Now suppose a company is consistently delivering a 50% return on equity, but recent events mean that a 40% return on equity is now perceived as more realistic. Even though a 40% rate of return may still be considered very good, the share price will fall.

This suggests that if you want to maximize the returns on the shares that you buy, don't look for the companies

that are already deemed to be delivering optimal performance – look for those where you believe return on
equity could potentially improve in the future. An adage I
often quote is: "A good company is not necessarily a good
investment."

The second point to note is that companies that are
underperforming (whether they are still fledgling businesses or have experienced recent trading difficulties) can
provide significant potential capital gains. Such companies
can readily be identified because they will typically have
market to book ratios that are well below those of their
peers. We noted in the table linking profit forecasts and
share prices that revising expectations of the future return
on equity from 5% to 10% results in the share price doubling. By contrast, revising expectations from a 15% return
on equity up to 20% only increases the share price by 33%.
In both cases managers are improving how effectively they
are using shareholders' funds by a full 5 percentage points,
but it is the company that is underperforming that will see
the most aggressive growth in its share price.

This is not a theory, it is a mathematical fact. It tells
us that if you want to make the maximum gains on shares,
you should seek out companies that appear not to be
doing so well at present. In other words, you are looking
for recovery or emerging stocks – companies that are either
struggling but will hopefully turn around their fortunes in
the not too distant future, or companies that are still in
their early stages of development but could surprise the
market when their true potential is realized. This is value
investing and, as already mentioned, some of the world's
most successful investors have made their fortunes pursuing this strategy. Bear in mind, however, that you are making a judgment call here – the market is not expecting the

company to do well in the future, but you are. The key point is, if you believe you have spotted a company with potential that the market has not, act fast: don't wait for the good news to break, because then it will be too late.

Given what I have just said, it follows that high returns are not easily achievable when a company is already doing well. Such companies will typically have high market to book ratios relative to their peers. Inevitably a point will be reached in any company's evolution where it is almost impossible to improve performance. Such companies will still witness share price growth as the wealth of the business increases, but not as much as companies that are emerging or are expected to deliver a business turnaround; in this instance, emphasis will tend to be placed on dividend growth. Growth investors are trying to find companies that typically already have sound market to book ratios but, given their well-established track record, still have potential to grow further.

Does this mean that if you are a value investor you simply need to find companies with low market to book ratios, while if you are a growth investor you are looking for companies with a more robust ratio? Definitely not. It's time to introduce what I call the **50% rule**. According to this rule, when somebody sells a share, somebody else must be buying it. This implies that somebody is saying "great time to sell," while somebody else is saying "great time to buy" – so 50% of the market must always be wrong. It's a simplistic view and takes no account of the various motivations underpinning why people buy and sell shares at a particular point in time, but it does introduce a useful discipline to adopt whenever you want to trade.

If you want to buy a tranche of shares because you believe they are cheap, how come other people exist who

are so willing to sell them to you? Do they know something you don't? If everyone thought they were cheap, they
would be buying them and the price would be soaring.
Similarly, if you decide it is time to sell some shares (maybe
you believe the price has peaked), how come other people
are prepared to buy them? All the 50% rule is really saying
is that you should always have the discipline to question
why a share appears cheap or why it appears expensive.

Before moving on, special mention needs to be made
of companies whose market to book ratio gets close to, or
even falls below, 1. Once the ratio falls below 1, the book
value of the company is greater than the market value.
In other words, the net assets of the business are more
valuable than the business itself. This is when businesses
become most vulnerable to a takeover and all of a sudden
the vultures appear.

One of two motivations tends to lie behind most acqui-
sitions in this circumstance. Either the acquiring business
has a strategy to rebuild the company, or it wants to break
up the business and sell off the assets (this is called asset
stripping). Even in the absence of a takeover, asset stripping
may still take place, as companies sell off assets in order
to raise cash. Furthermore, a market to book ratio that is
consistently below 1 may be a precursor to business failure.

As always, share dealing all comes down to expectations of the future. If you find a company with a market to
book ratio close to or less than 1, there may be an opportunity for a significant capital gain if the business is able
to turn itself around or it can be bought out at a premium.
However, it could also create a significant loss for you if
the business degenerates further or even ceases trading.

It should now be evident that the reward stage – estimating the potential rewards from shares – is somewhat

intricate. In the previous chapter we were introduced to return on equity, which assesses how shareholders' funds have been managed in the past. In this chapter we have been discussing the market to book ratio, which focuses attention on how effectively shareholders' funds are expected to be managed in the future. To help you in your decision-making, I have created an analytical device called a **value matrix**, which brings these two measures together to build an overall picture of a company's trading potential. It links the returns being achieved in the past (as reflected in the annual report) to the returns being anticipated in the future (as reflected in the share price). By simply drawing a graph that plots the relationship between return on equity and the market to book ratio, four distinct quadrants are created.

Return on equity	QUADRANT 3 High return on equity Low market to book "Falling star"	QUADRANT 1 High return on equity High market to book "Shining star"
	QUADRANT 4 Low return on equity Low market to book "Space dust"	QUADRANT 2 Low return on equity High market to book "Rising star"

Market to book

THE VALUE MATRIX

The first challenge is to appreciate what is meant by a high and a low return on equity and what is meant by a high and a low market to book ratio. We know that a market to book ratio of less than 1 is indicative of a company that is expected to deliver returns that are below the market rate, whereas a value above 1 indicates a company expected to deliver above-average market returns. So for the purposes of the value matrix, a low market to book ratio is where the value is 1 or less, while a high ratio is deemed to be where the value is over 1.

Turning our attention to return on equity, we noted in the previous chapter that most companies demand a rate of return that is at least double what could be achieved on long-term cash deposits. Building on this piece of logic, we noted that anything below 10% per annum is commonly regarded as a low return on equity. Not surprisingly, then, when constructing a value matrix it is common practice to set the breakpoint for return on equity at 10%. Any rate of return of 10% or less is deemed low, while any rate in excess of 10% is deemed high.

Do feel free to adjust the breakpoint for return on equity to whatever you deem to be appropriate for the stock exchange on which you intend to trade, but the principles underpinning the matrix remain unchanged. As soon as you have defined the breakpoints for the two measures, every company can be placed into one of the quadrants.

If a company is in Quadrant 1, it has been producing healthy rates of return on shareholders' funds in the past (as indicated by a high return on equity) and the high share price (as indicated by a high market to book ratio) suggests that this will continue in the future. These tend to be well-established, reliable companies and are commonly chosen by investors looking for reasonable future share price growth coupled with (where appropriate) reliable dividends. It is this quadrant that particularly attracts growth investors. These companies are what I call "shining stars."

A company in Quadrant 2 has not been producing healthy rates of return on shareholders' funds in the past (return on equity is low), but the share price suggests that performance will improve in the future (the market to book ratio is high). These tend to be slightly higher-risk companies than those in Quadrant 1, but can offer the opportunity for significant capital gains if the market has not yet recognized their full potential. These are what I call "rising stars."

A company in Quadrant 3 has been producing healthy rates of return on shareholders' funds in the past (as indicated by a high return on equity), but the share price suggests that performance is expected to deteriorate in the future (as indicated by a low market to book ratio). These companies offer significant capital gains if the market turns out to be wrong, but they are more risky than Quadrant 2 companies, as in buying them you are taking the view that the current market sentiment is misguided. These are what I call "falling stars."

A company in Quadrant 4 has not been producing healthy rates of return on shareholders' funds in the past (return on equity is low) and the share price suggests that the situation is not expected to change in the foreseeable future (the market to book ratio is low). These companies can sometimes produce spectacular capital gains if the market turns out to be wrong, but they also present the highest risk. Investors in these companies are often looking for recovery stocks (businesses that are struggling but have the ability to turn their fortunes around) and the quadrant is of particular interest to value investors. These companies are what I call "space dust."

In the previous chapter we saw how return on equity can be readily worked out from an annual report. In this chapter we have seen how, by combining the current share price with the book value per share (which again can be easily worked out), the market to book ratio can also be readily identified. You should be able to perform these calculations yourself in a matter of minutes, but if that seems like too much effort, there are many investment websites that report return on equity and market to book ratios for publicly owned companies. For example, Insight Investing provides a summary of all the key measures introduced in this chapter. This information is provided for every major company listed on the London Stock Exchange and it even states which quadrant of the value matrix the company falls within. We noted in the previous chapter that this website also provides a return on equity flowchart for each company.

We are now in a position to add some structure to the reward stage of the 6R approach. Having identified a potential investment opportunity in Stage 1:

∗   Create a return on equity flowchart and look at the interest cover and dividend cover to assess how effectively the business is being managed.

If you are happy with the management:

∗   Identify which quadrant within the value matrix the company currently resides.

COMPANY DETAILS

Name	EasyJet
Ticker	EZJ
Sector	Travel & Leisure

SHARE PRICE PERFORMANCE

Share price as at 24th March 2014	£16.22
Performance over last year:	
Share price growth	57.3%
Dividend yield	2.1%
Total shareholder return	59.4%
P/E	16.0
Market to book	3.2
Consensus	Hold
Insight rating	Quadrant 1 ⬆
Insight valuation	Fairly valued

INSIGHT INVESTING: SHARE PRICE PERFORMANCE

If it is a quadrant that is consistent with the type of opportunity you are looking for:

*   Compare your forecasted market to book ratio against the current market to book ratio to assess the share price.

Doing this should provide you with a reasonable feel for whether or not this is an opportunity that is worth pursuing further.

One final point: always consider the impact of tax on your returns. This will vary from one country to another, but don't forget that every dollar the government receives is a dollar you have lost. Check to see if there are any tax-efficient or tax-free investment vehicles available. For example, in many countries building a fund for retirement can attract tax breaks, while still allowing you to invest directly in financial securities such as shares.

Stage 3 – Risk

There are two main risks associated with shares:

* Capital loss.
* Income loss.

A capital loss can arise when the value of shares falls, resulting in a potential loss of some or all of your investment. You can also lose income since dividends are not guaranteed. This might suggest to the uninitiated that investing in shares is a very risky business, yet billions of dollars are invested in shares every day and it need not be anywhere near as risky as it is often portrayed. In fact, there are three ways to reduce the risks significantly:

* Think long term.
* Diversify.
* Understand company fundamentals.

First of all, you can reduce the risk by viewing shares as a long-term investment. This simple course of action immediately reduces the impact of short-term price fluctuations. To appreciate this, let us look at the share price of a company over a number of years.

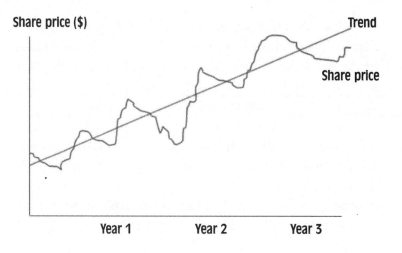

SHARE PRICES CAN BE VOLATILE IN THE SHORT TERM

You can see that over the years the share price of this company is gradually trending upward, while in the short term it fluctuates wildly around this trend. Short-term fluctuations are the result of news continually permeating the market about how the company is expected to do in the future. Naturally enough this news, which might be nothing more than idle rumor, affects the share price. The long-term trend is created through the company's underlying fundamental wealth-creating abilities.

Clearly, there are opportunities to make money out of the short-term price volatility, but success or failure often comes down to being able to sense the mood of the market, which is notoriously difficult. What we are concerned with here is maintaining risks within acceptable limits, and focusing attention on long-term prospects is one way of achieving this. When adopting this approach, if a share you are holding falls in price today, who cares? Relax – help yourself to a coffee and a doughnut. What matters is where you believe the share price is going to be in a year's time.

One other factor that needs to be taken into account that is directly linked to thinking long term is the timing of the purchase. To ensure that you are buying at the best price, it will help if you understand a little more about why share prices fluctuate around long-term trends.

One maxim that is commonly applied to shares is "Buy low, sell high." This is logical: if you want to make money on shares, you obviously want to sell them for more than you paid for them. Real life says that many investors do exactly the opposite. The following graph illustrates the cycle that many shares pass through in the long term.

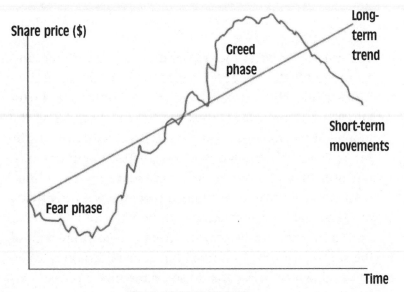

FEAR VERSUS GREED

When markets are booming and optimism is prevalent, share prices are high – because lots of people want to buy them. This is the greed phase, when investors believe that companies can do no wrong. They see returns increasing each year and want a piece of the action, so they clamber to buy shares and in so doing force prices up. When markets are depressed, share prices are low, because this is when lots of people want to sell. This is the fear phase, when investors can only see gloom and doom in the immediate future. They are tempted to sell their shares and in so doing force down share prices.

These fear and greed phases highlight that share performance is all about discipline versus emotion. When the market is depressed, lots of people want to sell. When the market is high, lots of people want to buy. It follows that the average person buys high and sells low and then seems surprised when they make losses! Why do this? It is where the crowds gather; it is what causes panic – fear and greed replace discipline. Although history confirms that this happens over and over again, people will always say: "This time it's different." Hence another adage I often quote: "If you follow the herd, take a shovel."

There is an oft-adopted principle called **contrarian investing**, which says that you should do exactly the opposite of what your emotions tell you to do. You should buy shares when markets are depressed, because that is when prices are low, and sell them when markets are buoyant, while prices are high. If you are investing for the long term and you want to maximize your returns, a great time to buy is during the fear phase when shares are relatively cheap. This does not mean that you should not buy shares during the greed phase, but do be wary. Bear in mind that it is notoriously difficult to spot the top or indeed the bottom of the market, so don't attempt it. What is far easier to sense is whether the market is in the fear phase or the greed phase, which will give you a sense of whether shares are generally underpriced or overpriced at the moment. The overriding message, though, is that if you want to reduce risk, think long term.

The second way to reduce risk is through diversification. Suppose you have $10,000 available to invest. Placing all your money into one company is high risk, as you are totally at the mercy of how that one company does in the future. A far lower-risk strategy is to invest $1,000 in ten different companies. Even if one of these companies turns out to be a disastrous investment, you still have nine others that can enhance your wealth. So you can reduce risk by investing in several companies rather than just one. Indeed, you can reduce risk even further by ensuring that the companies you select are in different industries.

You do not want to overdo diversification, however. It is often argued that extensive diversification is only appropriate when investors haven't got a clue what they are doing. You see, although diversification reduces risk, it also reduces the opportunity for high returns. The art of investing is spotting and exploiting opportunities as they arise. If you spread your investment over hundreds of companies and a couple of them turn out to be absolute gems, they will be such an insignificant part of your portfolio that the impact will be negligible. So do diversify, just don't overdo it. An ideal-sized portfolio should probably comprise between 20 and 30 companies.

GROW YOUR OWN MONEY

To reduce risk, always diversify your investment over several companies.

There is one other way to reduce risk: make sure that you understand the business and how it makes money. Study the return on equity flowchart of the company, along with its interest cover and dividend cover (as advocated during the previous stage of the 6R approach); look through its annual report to learn a little more about its products and services and its plans for the future; also read relevant news articles. These steps can all help improve your understanding of a company's trading capabilities. Does the company have a sound business model? Check the market it operates in; a company is only as good as the market it serves. Is it still likely to be trading in ten years' time? What are its potential strengths and weaknesses? Is the management team competent? How effectively is it managing the profit-making process? Has the company, or the industry in which it trades, been in the news recently? The more you know about the company, the more likely it is that you are going to make a sound investment decision.

One further point to note is that your style of investing can have an impact on risk. Value investors often claim that they have a greater margin of safety as the shares are already viewed unfavorably, so bad news does not have a great impact on the price, but they can respond very positively to good news. In contrast, growth stocks already have high expectations attached, so any disappointments can hit them hard. Growth investors counter this argument by saying that value investors tend to be commonly attracted to small or medium-sized companies, which may be less liquid, more risky, and more volatile.

It all comes down to what you feel most comfortable with. If you want solid reliable returns but are not concerned about achieving spectacular gains, be a growth investor. If you want more spice in your trading and are prepared to take on more risk, then being a value investor may well be more appropriate for you.

Stage 4 – Research

As with all wealth-creating assets, there are three other factors that need to be addressed when assessing a potential investment in shares: liquidity, term, and capital.

Most shares can be sold as and when required, so liquidity does not tend to be too much of an issue, but be aware that the timing of the sale may have an influence on the profit or loss that you make on the deal.

Moving on to term, we have noted that one way to reduce risk is to think long term and not get distracted by short-term fluctuations in the share price. This is also the stage when you should define your long-term objectives; in other words, decide when you intend to liquidate your shares. There tend to be three reasons to sell shares:

* The reason you were attracted to the share in the first place is no longer valid (e.g., yields have fallen).
* The share has met a long-term valuation target.
* Something better has come along.

Sometimes I buy shares with the specific objective of achieving a capital gain. In this situation I will set a long-term valuation target. For example, if I buy shares for $10 each and have decided that if I make a 30% return on the deal I'll be quite happy, the moment the share price hits $13 I sell. No emotion here. No thought as to whether the share price might increase further. I've achieved my objective and that is all that counts. All too often I encounter investors who have bought shares to achieve a capital gain, watched the share price increase, and then refuse to sell their holding because there was a possibility the share price would go even higher, only to witness it subsequently drop. As I often say: "Sometimes the mark of a successful investor is someone who is seen to sell too soon!"

> GROW YOUR OWN MONEY
> **Before buying shares, always have an exit strategy.**

The other issue that needs to be addressed before parting with your money is the amount of capital you require. There does not tend to be a minimum transaction size in share dealing: you can buy a single share for just a few dollars if you so wish. What is relevant here is the dealing charge, the fee you must pay to execute a buy or sell instruction.

Suppose you are being charged $10 per transaction. That means that you will pay $10 when you buy the shares and $10 when you sell them ($20 in total). In this circumstance you probably would not want to buy $100 worth of shares, because 20% of this would be eaten up by trading fees alone. Personally I like to keep trading fees at a maximum of 1% of the investment, so in this instance I would set the minimum investment at $2,000. Obviously, it is up to you how much of your investment you are happy to see eroded by trading fees; just bear in mind that every dollar you are paying in fees is a dollar you are failing to invest.

Stage 5 – Review

Share dealing is all about *anticipation*. A good footballer is not someone who runs to where the ball currently is; a good footballer will run to where the ball is going to be. In the same way, you should not invest in shares based on what they are doing now – you should invest in shares based on what you see them doing in the future.

Bear this in mind when reviewing the results of the first four stages of the 6R approach:

* What is the mood of the market generally?
* Are stock market indices rising or falling?
* How does the market feel about the company's prospects?
* Where is the share price relative to its 52-week high and its 52-week low?
* How do the yield and P/E look?
* How effectively has the company been managing the profit-making process?
* What is the interest cover and what is the dividend cover?
* What does the market to book ratio tell you about anticipated future trading?
* Within which quadrant in the value matrix does the company currently sit?
* How does your forecasted market to book ratio compare against the current market to book ratio?
* Has there been any breaking news regarding trading prospects for this company?
* If you are a value investor, why do you believe that the share is undervalued?
* If you are a growth investor, why do you believe that the company has potential to grow further?
* Are you prepared to invest for the long term?
* Which part of the long-term cycle is the economy in?
* Will this share purchase form part of a diversified portfolio?

Having addressed all of these issues, if you still believe that the share is a viable investment opportunity, only now should you be prepared to part with your cash.

So how do you open a share-dealing account? It is a straightforward process. Most banks offer an execution-only share-dealing service, via which they will buy and sell shares for you without providing any advice. In addition, there are many online share-dealing services. Having found a provider, you will normally be asked to nominate a bank account to which you want your share-dealing account to be linked. In order to buy shares you simply move funds from your bank account into your share-dealing account. When you sell shares, you can move the funds (if you do not intend to reinvest the proceeds) out of your trading account back into your bank account. The company providing the trading account will maintain your shareholding electronically and you can usually access your account online at any time to see what shares you currently hold, how much you paid for them, your gains and losses, dividends received, and so on.

Do be prepared to shop around. In particular, when selecting a provider watch out for the fees, which can vary dramatically from one provider to the next. In addition to fees for buying and selling, some brokerages also charge a monthly or quarterly fee for using their service. Incidentally, for those who don't like technology, telephone share-dealing services are also available, but the associated trading fees do tend to be a little more expensive.

Stage 6 – Revisit

It is easy to get facts, but facing those facts may prove to be somewhat more difficult. Review your portfolio regularly – monthly should be adequate for most people – and be prepared to listen to the market. You may invest in a company because you believe you know better than most people, but if the share price keeps falling maybe the market knows something that you don't.

Don't be frightened of losses – it's all part of investing in shares. If your shares aren't performing as expected, be prepared to move your money into alternative shares (or even alternative investments altogether).

THE ESSENTIALS

* **RECOGNIZE** – check financial indices. Identify a company that interests you. Examine the share price in the context of 52-week highs and lows, yields, and P/Es.
* **REWARD** – construct a return on equity flowchart. Identify trends in return on equity, gearing, asset turnover, and profit margin. Check the interest cover and dividend cover. Read news articles. Look at the market to book ratio. Consider the value matrix. Does the share price appear to be undervalued or overvalued?
* **RISK** – think long term. Spread your investments. Make sure that you understand the business you are thinking of investing in.
* **RESEARCH** – consider liquidity, term, and capital. Decide on an exit strategy. In what circumstances would you sell?
* **REVIEW** – do these shares meet your needs?
* **REVISIT** – remain vigilant. Review your shares on a regular basis. Be prepared to take action if they are not performing as expected.

9

BRICKS DON'T FLOAT:

INVESTING IN PROPERTY

Property is perceived by many as a straight-forward investment and they therefore mistakenly assume that there is very little they need to know. It is the very fact that property is an easy investment to understand that creates the greatest problem – people oversimplify it. It is true that it is not complicated and that serious money can be made investing in property, provided that you know what you are doing. Unfortunately, you can lose a lot as well. Even seasoned property investors with years of experience have sometimes watched their fortunes rapidly dissipate.

The main attraction of property is that the potential rewards are, as a general rule, significantly better than those provided by savings accounts. Indeed, the rewards can potentially be the highest on offer from any of the big four wealth-creating assets – but at a cost. Unlike shares, where there are plenty of opportunities to diversify your investment both across companies and across sectors, property invariably demands a significant investment in a single asset. Even if you invest in several properties, you are still relying on the performance of a single sector to generate your wealth. If the property market crashes, as it has done on numerous occasions, the losses you could incur may prove to be very significant indeed. Not surprisingly, all the hard work should take place *before* you ever part with your money. Once you have bought a property, if it turns out you have made a poor decision, it is very hard to rectify the problem. Consequently, successful property investment is all about planning.

As with the other investment opportunities, the 6R approach can be applied.

Stage 1 – Recognize

There are two ways in which investing in property can make your money grow:

* The value of the property can go up.
* You can generate income by renting out the property.

Your first challenge is to decide how you want to grow your money. In other words, what sort of participant do you want to be in this market? This will determine your approach to property investing. If you want to be a property trader or a property developer you will be adopting the buy to sell approach to making money, whereas if you want to be a landlord you will be adopting the buy to rent approach.

You also need to decide what sort of property you want to invest in. You have two options:

* Residential property.
* Commercial property.

This comes down to who you want your customers to be. With residential property you are selling or renting to individuals, whereas with commercial property your customers are businesses. In many ways the two types of property are similar, but there are two fundamental differences. First is the price: commercial properties tend to be in a higher price bracket, which is often due to the fact they are considerably bigger. Then, if you intend to be a landlord, there is the tenancy issue. Tenancies of several years are not uncommon for commercial properties, compared with maybe just a few months for a residential tenant. A key advantage of commercial property, then, if you are a landlord, is that it can provide a much more predictable income stream.

Only after addressing these issues should you go out and look for appropriate investment opportunities.

Stage 2 – Reward

The reward you can achieve from property investment will depend on the approach that you are adopting.

Starting with the buy-to-sell approach, the basics are easy to understand. Ideally, you want to buy at a low price and sell at a high price, leaving you with a nice big profit. This approach is all about capital growth, as there is no income involved. Unfortunately, once you scratch away at the surface, it soon becomes apparent that it is not as straightforward as might at first appear. The process can be broken down into three stages:

* Buy.
* Hold.
* Sell.

Each stage has associated costs that erode your potential profit, so it is essential that you fully appreciate the impact that they have on performance. These three stages apply whether you are a trader or a developer.

The most obvious buying cost is the purchase price of the property. How much you are prepared to pay will depend on whether you are a trader or a developer. If you are a trader you are looking for a property that is available at below market value (as might be the case when a vendor needs a quick sale). A developer, by contrast, may be quite happy to pay the market price for a site provided that it has potential for yielding a profit in the future. In addition to the purchase price, there are other buying costs that must be accounted for, such as legal fees and taxes.

Holding costs refer to those incurred while you own the property. For a trader, the most significant holding cost will probably be the mortgage interest (assuming that a loan has been used to acquire the property in the first place). A developer will also suffer this cost, but in addition will have to allow for all the anticipated costs of building or renovating the property. When dealing with any form of development project, it is always good practice to include a contingency fund to cater for any unexpected events. Also watch out for budget creep, where you pay a little extra here and there and before you know it, all the potential profit has gone. Remember, the only person that suffers when the budget is overspent is you.

Finally there are selling costs, which include expenses such as sales agency fees and legal fees.

Once these costs have been identified, the potential profit on the deal can be estimated by taking the projected sales proceeds and deducting the buying, holding, and selling costs.

Suppose there is a property available for purchase for $200,000 with additional buying costs estimated at $10,000. You anticipate holding costs of $120,000, comprising $105,000 to renovate the property plus $15,000

set aside for contingencies. The anticipated selling price is
$400,000, with selling costs likely to be $30,000. Based
on these figures we can identify the anticipated profit by
preparing an income statement, which simply involves
deducting the various costs from the sales figure.

INCOME STATEMENT

	$
SALES PROCEEDS	**400,000**
LESS	
Buying costs:	
Purchase price of property	−200,000
Additional buying costs	−10,000
Holding costs:	
Renovation costs	−105,000
Contingency	−15,000
Selling costs	−30,000
PROFIT	40,000

ASSESSING A POTENTIAL BUY TO SELL DEAL

Based on projected sales proceeds of $400,000 and pro-
jected costs of $360,000, a profit of $40,000 is anticipated.
What matters to an investor, though, is not the monetary
profit – it is the rate of return that counts. This can be calculated by taking the profit figure and expressing it as a
percentage of the funds invested.

KEY MEASURE

$$\text{Rate of return on buy to sell deal} = \frac{\text{Profit on sale}}{\text{Amount invested}} \times 100\%$$

If you are obliged to pay out all buying, holding, and selling costs prior to receiving the sales proceeds, the value of your investment is equivalent to the total expenditure of $360,000. However, if you are only liable to pay certain costs at the point of sale or even after the sale takes place (sales agency fees might fall into this category), then these costs can be excluded from the value of your investment.

For the purposes of this example, we are going to assume that all costs are payable prior to the sale taking place. Based on this assumption, the potential rate of return is as follows:

$$\text{Rate of return on buy to sell deal} = \frac{\text{Profit on sale of }\$40,000}{\text{Investment of }\$360,000} \times 100\%$$

$$= 11\%$$

This particular property is offering the potential to earn a return of 11%, which may seem okay. Yet property has a reputation for delivering potentially very high returns indeed and 11% is really not in the super league. The real attraction of property to the seasoned investor is the opportunity to improve this rate of return significantly. What is about to follow is by far the most exciting part of this chapter!

If you have savings accounts, one way to potentially improve your rate of return is to use your savings to reduce your debts. Property works in exactly the opposite way. Regardless of whether you are a trader, a developer, or a landlord, increasing debt can increase your rate of return. Debt is at the very heart of property investment. Use debt wisely and it can unlock huge returns, but use it recklessly and you can lose a fortune.

Many investors are attracted to property simply because in the long term it is often perceived as a sound investment, with property price increases tending to out-strip inflation. Suppose you see a house that will cost you $200,000 to buy and that you believe will increase in value over the next year by 10%. To keep things simple, we will assume that there are no further buying, holding, or sell-ing costs. The intention is to buy the property using your own money in the hope of selling it for $220,000 in one year's time, providing you with a handsome $20,000 profit on the deal. Given that you are having to invest $200,000, a $20,000 profit represents a 10% return on your invest-ment. So in this example, the rate of return you achieve on the property is equivalent to the rate at which property prices are increasing. Based on this principle, if property prices are increasing by 10% a year while inflation is only 5% per year, many individuals would regard this as a suffi-cient incentive to invest, but a serious investor will always be looking for ways to improve the rate of return.

Suppose property prices are indeed increasing by 10% per annum, but you would like to earn more. How can you increase the rate of return? This is where you meet your new best friend, debt, which can increase your rate of return substantially.

Instead of financing the entire deal yourself, you decide to approach a bank and take out a $180,000 mort-gage at the outset. The problem with doing this is that you have to pay interest on the loan. If the annual loan rate is 5%, the amount of interest you will end up paying during the year will be $9,000. This means that out of the $20,000 increase in property value, there is a new holding cost that must be allowed for of $9,000, which will go to the bank in the form of interest, thereby reducing your profit to $11,000. You may well be thinking that this is significantly less than in the previous scenario, so what's the point?

It is time to look at the rate of return. In order to do this, we need to identify how much you have invested in the project. Given that the bank is providing $180,000 toward the purchase price, your personal investment is only $20,000. In addition to this, while you own the property, you will need to inject a further $9,000 to pay the interest on the loan, so your total investment over the next 12 months will be $29,000. Having identified this figure, we can work out your rate of return:

$$\text{Rate of return on buy to sell deal} = \frac{\text{Profit on sale of \$11,000}}{\text{Investment of \$29,000}} \times 100\%$$

$$= 38\%$$

Congratulations, you have just increased your rate of return from 10% to 38% and all you have done, in order to achieve this, is borrowed money. This is how to make serious money out of property and it is this principle that has resulted in the creation of many property millionaires.

The other approach to property investment is buy to rent – purchasing a property with the intention of holding on to it in order to generate rental income. This yields two potential benefits: income and capital growth. Consequently, this approach is a little more involved than buy to sell. The first intricacy is encountered at the outset when you need to determine what your goals are. You have two options:

* Income only.
* Income and capital growth.

The income-only option means that the objective is to generate a healthy income stream, with any capital appreciation being regarded as a bonus. If you are pursuing both income and capital growth, the objective is to generate a healthy income stream for a while, prior to the property being sold. We'll start with income generation, as this is relevant to all types of landlord.

Being a landlord is all about generating a positive cash flow each year: ensuring that the cash you receive exceeds the cash you pay out. Two measures exist in the property world to ensure that this is happening:

* Gross yield.
* Net yield.

If you don't know the difference between the two you're definitely in the wrong game, so let's sort out the distinction here and now.

Gross yield is calculated by dividing the annual rent by the current market value of the property.

KEY MEASURE

$$\text{Gross yield} = \frac{\text{Annual rent}}{\text{Property value}} \times 100\%$$

If rent from a property is \$32,000 and the current value of the property is \$400,000, the gross yield can be worked out as follows:

$$\text{Gross yield} = \frac{\text{Annual rent of \$32,000}}{\text{Property value of \$400,000}} \times 100\%$$

$$= 8\%$$

On every $100 currently tied up in the property, rent of $8 is being generated each year. This provides an effective method for estimating the rental income from any buy to rent property: simply multiply the property value by the expected gross yield.

KEY MEASURE
Estimated rental income = Property value x Expected gross yield

You are looking to buy a property for $500,000 and you have been advised by a local property agent that gross yields in the area are typically around 6%. This is valuable information as it enables you to estimate what the annual rental will be:

Estimated rental income
= Property value of $500,000 x Expected gross yield of 6%
= $30,000

Even though you have not bought the property yet, you have already established that you should expect an annual rental income of around $30,000. This should be the starting point when looking at acquiring any potential buy to rent property and a little research should lead you to this information fairly easily. Insight Investing provides regular updates on price movements and gross yields for properties in the UK.

Regional Performance

As at 24th March 2014

REGION	ANNUAL PRICE CHANGE %		ANNUAL GROSS RENTAL YIELD %		ANNUAL TOTAL RETURN %
▶ North East	3.0	+	4.6	=	7.6
▶ North West	3.5	+	5.0	=	8.5
▶ Yorkshire & Humberside	1.8	+	4.5	=	6.3
▶ East Midlands	1.9	+	4.4	=	6.3
▶ West Midlands	4.3	+	4.4	=	8.7
▶ East	4.6	+	4.1	=	8.7
▶ London	12.3	+	4.6	=	16.9
▶ South East	3.8	+	4.0	=	7.8
▶ South West	2.5	+	4.5	=	7.0
▶ England	5.7	+	4.4	=	10.1
▶ Wales	4.8	+	4.7	=	9.5
▶ Scotland	0.5	+	4.4	=	4.9
▶ Northern Ireland	4.8	+	5.5	=	10.3
▶ United Kingdom	5.5	+	4.5	=	10.0

Data Sources: HomeLet, Office for National Statistics

Analysis: Insight Financial Consulting

INSIGHT INVESTING: PROPERTY DATA

Although gross yield is of interest, it is not much use when it comes to assessing the viability of a rental property. Properties do not look after themselves; it is ultimately down to you to maintain the property and doing this costs money. What is far more relevant in this respect is net yield.

Unlike gross yield, which only considers rental income, **net yield** also takes account of operating costs and thereby provides an indication of the potential profitability of a property. It is calculated by deducting the annual operating costs from the annual rent and then dividing the answer by the value of the property.

KEY MEASURE

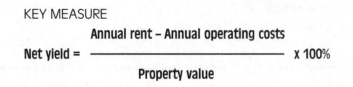

$$\text{Net yield} = \frac{\text{Annual rent} - \text{Annual operating costs}}{\text{Property value}} \times 100\%$$

Annual operating costs in this context include normal everyday expenses that you would associate with running a rental property, such as insurance, rental agency fees, decorating, and maintenance. There is one cost that is always omitted, though: loan interest. Interest is determined by how you finance the property; it has nothing to do with the running of the property itself.

Returning to our earlier example, where the rent is $32,000 per annum and the property is worth $400,000, suppose the annual operating costs are expected to be $8,000. This is all you need to know to calculate net yield:

Net yield

$$= \frac{\text{Annual rent of } \$32,000 - \text{Annual operating costs of } \$8,000}{\text{Property value of } \$400,000} \times 100\%$$

$$= \frac{\$24,000}{\$400,000} \times 100\%$$

$$= 6\%$$

On every $100 invested in the property, you can earn an annual profit of $6 before paying any interest on loans. This is the rate of return that you can anticipate in terms of rental income on your $400,000 investment, with any capital gain being additional to this. If you are happy with this figure, then the investment may well be viable.

We have already seen how borrowing money can significantly improve the rate of return achieved on a buy to sell deal. You will no doubt be delighted to hear that the same principle can be employed to improve your rate of return when adopting the buy to rent approach.

Let's stick with the latest example. Suppose you decide to borrow $360,000 to purchase the property at an annual loan rate of 5%, so the interest charge each year will be $18,000. This means that you are now only having to invest $40,000 of your own money. The annual rent is still $32,000 and the associated operating costs are $8,000. The rate of return is worked out by deducting the operating costs and loan interest from the annual rent to determine the profit being made, which is then expressed as a percentage of the money invested.

KEY MEASURE

$$\text{Rate of return on buy to rent deal} = \frac{\begin{array}{c}\text{Annual rent}\\ \text{– Annual operating costs}\\ \text{– Annual interest payable}\end{array}}{\text{Amount invested}} \times 100\%$$

In this instance, the rate of return works out as follows:

$$\text{Rate of return} = \frac{\begin{array}{c}\text{Annual rent of \$32,000}\\ \text{– Annual operating costs of \$8,000}\\ \text{– Annual interest payable of \$18,000}\end{array}}{\text{Investment of \$40,000}} \times 100\%$$

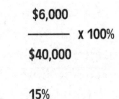

$$= \frac{\$6,000}{\$40,000} \times 100\%$$

$$= 15\%$$

Although the net yield on the property is 6%, you are managing to achieve a rate of return of 15%. Once again, this has been achieved by borrowing money. It should be noted that, when looking at the value of the investment in a buy to rent deal, loan interest is not included (unlike in a buy to sell deal where it is included). This is because it will be paid out of the rental income during the year and therefore does not demand any additional financial commitment on the part of the landlord.

What we have looked at so far is how to evaluate a buy to rent deal assuming that your only objective is to generate income, but you may be entering the buy to rent market in the hope of achieving a capital gain as well. To identify the rate of return on a hybrid deal (where you are looking for both income and a capital gain), you need to introduce the increase in property value to the calculation.

KEY MEASURE

$$\text{Rate of return on hybrid deal} = \frac{\begin{array}{c}\text{Annual rent}\\ -\text{ Annual operating costs}\\ -\text{ Annual interest payable}\\ +\text{ Annual increase in property value}\end{array}}{\text{Amount invested}} \times 100\%$$

Staying with the latest example, assume that property prices are increasing by 4% per annum. This means that over the next year you would expect the value of the property to increase by $16,000, from $400,000 to $416,000. How would this affect the rate of return?

$$\text{Rate of return} = \frac{\begin{array}{l}\text{Annual rent of \$32,000} \\ -\text{ Annual operating costs of \$8,000} \\ -\text{ Annual interest payable of \$18,000} \\ +\text{ Annual increase in property value of \$16,000}\end{array}}{\text{Investment of \$40,000}} \times 100\%$$

$$= \frac{\$22,000}{\$40,000} \times 100\%$$

$$= 55\%$$

Although property prices are only increasing by 4% per annum and net yields are 6%, because you have borrowed money, your overall rate of return leaps up to 55%. Now that's a neat trick! I have to emphasize that this is an estimated rate of return. Strictly speaking, the calculation would have to be done for each year you intend to hold on to the property, because each year the property value would be increasing, which in turn would affect the value of your investment. Also, annual rentals and operating costs may alter. However, given that nobody knows for sure what property prices are going to do and all we want is an estimate, for this purpose the calculation is fine.

There is one other issue that needs to be addressed when looking at buy to rent deals specifically. If you are

seeking a potential capital gain on a property, in addition
to rental income, there is always the option to resort to
a strategy called **negative gearing** (not to be confused
with the term gearing that is used when looking at how
companies raise finance). Put simply, negative gearing
exists when rental income is insufficient to cover the loan
interest and operating costs; you will be paying out more
than you receive each year. Why are people prepared to get
themselves into this situation? If the annual rental income
is $10,000 less than the interest and operating costs com-
bined, but the property is increasing in value by $20,000
each year, although you may have less cash, your overall
wealth is still increasing. However, this is a far higher-risk
strategy than when you have a positive cash flow each year.

Anyone who adopts negative gearing is speculating
that the potential capital gain they will make on the property will more than outweigh the certain income loss in
the meantime. This is high risk indeed, but it can be useful
in certain circumstances, such as when property prices in
an area are steadily climbing but attainable rents are relatively low.

Tax can also have an impact on your rate of return, so
always check out the tax implications when considering
investing in property. Depending on the country in which
you reside, tax may be payable when you buy a property,
when you rent out a property, and when you sell a property.

Stage 3 – Risk

Unlike most other types of investment, property
demands a significant initial outlay. It is thus particularly
important that the risks should be fully appraised before
you ever let go of your cash.

When adopting the buy to sell approach, there are two risks:

* Property prices fall.
* Costs increase.

Regrettably, no matter how meticulous you are in calculating anticipated costs, the ability to make profit is entirely determined by the sales proceeds you receive. The problem is that the property market, like the share market, can be fickle: prices can go down as well as up. This is an issue whether you are a property trader or a property developer, but it is particularly acute if you are a developer, because there is usually a significant time gap between when the property is purchased and when it is sold. This is the main risk inherent in adopting the buy-to-sell approach, but fortunately it can be managed by examining the profit margin, which looks at the profit on the deal as a percentage of the sales proceeds.

KEY MEASURE

$$\text{Profit margin on buy to sell deal} = \frac{\text{Profit on sale}}{\text{Sales proceeds}} \times 100\%$$

Earlier in this chapter we considered a property that was going to cost $200,000, with the potential of being sold for $220,000 in a year's time. It was to be financed by a $180,000 loan, with you providing the remaining $20,000. The problem with doing this was that you would end up having to pay interest on the loan of $9,000, which would reduce your profit to $11,000. At the same time, we noted that your total investment would be $29,000 (comprising your $20,000 initial investment plus the loan interest of $9,000), giving an anticipated rate of return of 38% ($11,000 profit as a percentage of your $29,000 investment). Taking all of this into account you might be tempted to think, "Great, let's go for it!" But what about the risk?

Although making a profit of $11,000 on a $29,000 investment might sound appealing, when it comes to assessing risk, it is far more useful to look at the profit margin:

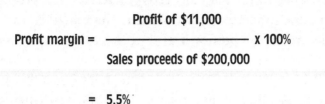

$$\text{Profit margin} = \frac{\text{Profit of \$11,000}}{\text{Sales proceeds of \$200,000}} \times 100\%$$

$$= 5.5\%$$

This tells us that if the selling price you achieve is more than 5.5% below what you have anticipated, you will end up making a loss. That throws a very different light on this particular opportunity; whether or not you proceed now comes down to your perception of risk. The larger the profit margin, the more chance there is that you will ultimately make a profit.

Deciding whether or not the margin is sufficient to minimize your risk will be influenced by whether you are a trader or a developer. As a general principle, a property trader will be willing to accept a narrower margin than a property developer. This is for two reasons: the time that elapses between purchase and sale is shorter, coupled with the fact that there are no estimated development costs to take account of.

GROW YOUR OWN MONEY
To assess the risk of a potential buy to sell deal, always calculate the profit margin.

With the buy to rent approach there are three things that can go wrong when it comes to generating a profitable income stream:

* Income falls.
* Yields fall.
* Costs increase.

When it comes to income, there may be times when you are unable to rent out the property or, even if you do, the tenant fails to pay the rent. As far as yields are concerned, even if they are attractive now, it does not necessarily follow that they will continue to be as healthy in the future. Furthermore, annual operating costs such as rental agency fees and maintenance might go up. You must examine each of these risks and decide whether or not they pose a realistic threat to the viability of the investment. Regrettably, there is no magical formula that will make this decision for you; it is down to your judgment. It is the ability to manage these risks that often separates the successful from the unsuccessful landlord.

Fortunately, there is a technique that will at least help quantify the risks, called **sensitivity analysis**. This comes in many guises as it has many differing applications, but essentially it is always doing the same thing: it looks at how sensitive the outcome of a project is to the assumptions being made. What we are going to consider now is a simple, but very powerful, application of this technique.

Let's return to the buy to rent example where you borrow $360,000 to purchase a $400,000 property. If you recall, interest payable during the year is $18,000, annual operating costs are $8,000, and annual rent is $32,000. Let's tabulate these results in an income statement.

	$	SENSITIVITY
RENTAL INCOME	32,000	19%
Operating costs	-8,000	75%
Interest payable	-18,000	33%
PROFIT	6,000	

USING SENSITIVITY ANALYSIS TO ASSESS RISK

In this statement the various costs have been deducted from the rental income in order to ascertain the profit. Of course, all these figures are estimates; they are what we expect to happen in the future and projections can be wrong. But how wrong can the estimates be before this property no longer generates a profit? The right-hand column entitled "Sensitivity" answers this question.

Starting with rental income, the forecast is $32,000. You can also see that, based on this figure, an annual profit of $6,000 is anticipated. It follows that if annual rental income fell by $6,000 to $26,000, profit would drop to zero. In other words, if rental income was 19% below expectations, the property would no longer be profitable.

Exactly the same logic can be applied to operating costs. If operating costs were $6,000 higher than the $8,000 estimate, once again, profit would fall to zero; this represents an increase of 75%. Finally, if interest payable was $6,000 higher than the $18,000 estimate, once again profit would fall to zero, which is a 33% increase.

What sensitivity analysis is getting you to do is to challenge your estimates. Could you be out by more than 19% on your estimated rental income, or by more than 75% on your estimated operating costs, or by more than 33% on your estimated interest payable? Just by looking at these percentages you can see that the greatest risk surrounds the rental income. You need to be pretty confident about this figure if you are going to proceed with this opportunity. In this particular example you have the luxury of a 19% margin of error, which many landlords may feel is well within their comfort zone. However, if the margin of error was only 4%, you would need to be very cautious indeed if you were to progress this any further.

GROW YOUR OWN MONEY

To assess the risk of a potential buy to rent deal, always apply sensitivity analysis to your rental income and cost estimates.

One risk that has been omitted from this discussion is the possibility of a fall in the value of the property itself. This is deliberate. If you are buying a property purely to generate income, changes in its market value are only relevant inasmuch as they affect rental income. However, it may be that you only intended to generate income for a while and a disposal was always part of the plan. If this is the case, attention now needs to turn to maximizing the capital gain.

Logically, if you want to maximize your capital gain, you want to buy when house prices are at their lowest. Unfortunately, spotting when the market is bottoming out is notoriously difficult. What is easier to spot is when the market is weak; in other words, when house prices seem significantly lower than they were previously. Many people are put off buying property at this stage due to the fear of prices falling even further. Don't let this deter you. Yes, there is always a risk that this could happen, but the good news is that any fall in property prices can be combated by the fact that you only suffer a financial loss when you dispose of the property, so falling prices may not turn out to be a problem at all.

Suppose you buy a house for $200,000, which then drops in value to $190,000 over the next couple of years. Although you would make a loss if you sold at this stage, the critical issue is whether or not the house will increase in value in the future. If it climbs in value to $260,000 a couple of years later, you will still make a profit on the deal. Indeed, if you have got your net yield calculations right, you will enjoy a healthy income over the full four years with the added bonus of a decent capital gain at the end.

Property markets go through cycles. There will be periods of gradual (or not so gradual) price increases followed by periods of falling prices. The same property can enjoy continually changing valuations over the years. Consequently, achieving a healthy capital gain is all about timing: get the timing right and you could make a fortune; get it wrong and the consequences could be dire. So are there any signals that can help you assess whether the market is booming or depressed?

When looking at shares, the P/E ratio can be used to provide an initial assessment of share prices, by considering the price of the share relative to its earnings. A high ratio suggests a buoyant share price (the price being significantly higher than the earnings), whereas a low ratio indicates a more pessimistic outlook. There is an equivalent measure applied in the property sector – the house price to earnings ratio, which considers average house prices relative to average earnings.

KEY MEASURE

$$\text{House price to earnings} = \frac{\text{Average house price}}{\text{Average earnings}}$$

This measure is often used to help explain the cyclical nature of house prices. When property prices are low relative to household earnings, property is easily affordable. New buyers enter the market and prices start to increase. Now comes the unfortunate twist, which is what leads to housing bubbles. According to basic economic theory, as prices of goods and services increase, demand falls. This applies in most situations, but not to property. When property prices increase, demand also increases: the more expensive houses become, the more people want them. This behavior is led by confusion: homeowners are unable to distinguish between homes and investments. Property is no longer just somewhere to live, it is viewed as a means of increasing wealth. The higher prices go, the more attractive the investment appeal of property becomes.

Ultimately, a point is reached at which the price of housing, relative to earnings, is no longer sustainable. Property prices fall until house prices relative to income appear good value again. Buyers reenter the market and so the cycle starts all over again. Consequently, the house price to earnings ratio can provide a useful indicator of when the market is depressed and when it is booming.

Of course, you will not ever need to work out this ratio, as it is readily available on the internet and in investment publications. The basic rule of thumb runs as follows. When the house price to earnings ratio is significantly below its long-term average, the market is depressed, whereas when it is significantly above its long-term average, the market is buoyant. What this measure cannot tell you is when the market has reached its low point and is about to turn around, or when the bubble is about to burst.

This discussion does not mean that you cannot make money out of property – many people do and this chapter would be a waste of time if property did not provide an opportunity to grow your wealth. What it does mean, however, is that there is a stark distinction between property investors and the average person on the street who simply believes that property is a good investment. A property investor, as has been emphasized throughout this chapter, appreciates the importance of planning. A property investor will carefully prepare revenue and cost estimates, assess the risk inherent in those estimates, and, if the plans don't look as if they will realistically deliver a healthy return, walk away from the deal. Somebody who simply believes that property is a good investment will part with their money regardless, in the mistaken belief that property prices can only go up. The credit crunch provided a stark reminder of what can happen when such a belief is perpetuated.

Stage 4 – Research

Liquidity is a particularly pertinent issue when it comes to investing in property. Selling a property can be a long drawn-out process, so if you need ready access to cash, property is not an appropriate wealth-creating asset. Having to dispose of a property in a hurry can result in you having to sell at substantially below market value, which could cost you dear.

Moving on to term, traders can anticipate substantial returns within a matter of months, as can property developers, although development of a property can add to the delay in achieving returns. As a landlord, you can start to generate rents almost immediately, although you will not have access to your capital for many years.

On the capital issue, unlike the other big four wealth-creating assets, property usually demands a substantial investment in a single asset. This not only means that your returns are contingent on how this single asset performs, but also precludes you from taking advantage of other investment opportunities that may arise prior to any sale.

Stage 5 – Review

Take a reality check – this is the most important step of all. You are about to invest a significant sum in a single asset. Optimism has no role here; what is required at this stage is realism.

* How realistic are your revenue and cost estimates?
* What is the potential rate of return?
* Could taking on debt improve the potential rate of return?
* If it is a buy to sell deal, what is the profit margin?
* If it is a buy to rent deal, does sensitivity analysis reveal any particular areas of concern?
* Is the house price to earnings ratio for the area above or below its long-term average?
* Are you prepared to tie up a significant sum for several months (if adopting the buy-to-sell approach)?
* Are you prepared to tie up a significant sum for several years (if adopting the buy-to-rent approach)?

All of these questions need to be addressed before you part with your money. Having reached this step, if you are still convinced that this particular property is the way forward, it may well be that there is an opportunity here for you to increase your wealth.

Stage 6 – Revisit

If you're a property trader, you need to ensure that your properties are being sold. If they are not, what can be done to attract more potential buyers?

If you're a property developer, it is essential that you review your costs regularly. Are costs within budget or are you becoming susceptible to budget creep? Also keep an eye on what is happening to property prices, as these will have a direct impact on the profit potential of any particular project.

If you're a landlord, you also need to manage costs carefully, but make sure that you are generating sufficient rental income as well. It is all very well having a tenant, but if they are not paying rent on time, what action are you taking to remedy the situation? Are you failing to obtain tenants? If so, why? More than with any other form of wealth-creating asset, you need to keep in touch with how this kind of investment is performing.

THE ESSENTIALS

✳ **RECOGNIZE** – decide whether you want to be a trader, developer, or landlord. Also decide whether you want to deal in residential or commercial property.

✳ **REWARD** – estimate the rate of return. Could borrowing improve the rate of return?

✳ **RISK** – if it's a buy to sell deal, check the profit margin. If it's a buy to rent deal, use sensitivity analysis to assess your rental income and cost estimates.

✳ **RESEARCH** – property is highly illiquid, demands significant capital investment, and (particularly if you're a landlord) should be viewed as a long-term investment.

✳ **REVIEW** – does this property meet your needs?

✳ **REVISIT** – given the sums involved, it is essential that you regularly review your projected revenue and cost streams.

10

YOU CAN'T WIN IF YOU DON'T PLAY

This is a short but important chapter: it consolidates everything that has been covered in the previous nine. I would like to think that at this stage you have picked up some key messages:

* If you want to maximize your returns, you have to take control and make your own investment decisions, because nobody cares more about your money than you do.
* In order to grow your own money you have to invest in wealth-creating assets, but there tends to be a tradeoff between rate of return and risk.
* In addition to risk, liquidity, term, and capital also need to be considered when assessing any investment opportunity.
* Compounding can significantly enhance the overall returns you achieve.
* The big four investment opportunities to grow your own money are savings accounts, bonds, shares, and property.
* The 6R approach provides a disciplined methodology for making any investment decision, ensuring that you take account of all the relevant facts.

In addition, hopefully you have gained an in-depth understanding of how each of the big four investment opportunities works in practice and how you as an independent investor can take advantage of them.

The most important message that you should take away from all of this is that investing is not difficult – the principles really are quite straightforward, and applying them need not be overly time consuming. However, if you want to be a successful independent investor, it is essential that you adopt a disciplined approach to every investment decision you make.

Nobody has become wealthy simply by reading a book: it is only by applying the knowledge that you can ever hope to grow your own money. Are you ready to take control and make your first key investment decision for real? Every day you are presented with a choice: Are you going to take action to grow your own money or not? If you want to improve your financial wellbeing, the first step begins when you wake up. Ask yourself this question every morning: "What am I going to do today to increase my wealth?" Too many people want to be better off and then fall at the first hurdle; they don't take time out to think about how they are going to do it and, not surprisingly, nothing happens.

What I am going to walk you through now is the course of action I pursued when I decided to become an independent investor. I urge you not just to read the next few pages, but also to let them spur you into action; believe me, the rewards are worth it. Replicating the journey I have been through will not make you rich beyond your wildest dreams, but it should place you in a position that will enable you to enhance your wealth significantly in the years to come.

Prepare a balance sheet

If you genuinely want to grow your own money, the first move is to construct a personal balance sheet. Add up everything you own and deduct everything you owe; this will tell you what you have now. Doing this once a year is a great way to monitor how your money is growing over time. It may seem a bit of a chore first time round, but I guarantee that in a year's time there will be no holding you back as you see how much your money has grown during the preceding 12 months.

Choose the wealth-creating assets that are right for you

Your next challenge is to decide which forms of wealth-creating asset best suit your requirements. Remember the main features of each of the big four investment opportunities, as outlined in Chapter 3. Only you can decide what sacrifices you are prepared to make to achieve the future returns on offer.

	Savings accounts	**Bonds**	**Shares**	**Property**
Return	Low	Medium	High	Very high
Liquidity	✔	✔	✔	✗
Risk	✔	✔	✗	✗
Term	✔	✗	✗	✗
Capital	✔	✗	✗	✗

✔ denotes that the issue is not usually significant
✗ denotes that the issue is always significant

THE BIG FOUR: KEY FEATURES COMPARED

Apply the 6R approach to your decision-making

Having identified the wealth-creating assets most appropriate to your needs, you now need to make some investment decisions, but it is essential that you are disciplined when doing this. The 6R approach provides structure to the decision-making process, ensuring that you systematically address each aspect of investing:

* Stage 1 – RECOGNIZE the opportunity.
* Stage 2 – Identify the potential REWARD.
* Stage 3 – Assess the RISK.
* Stage 4 – RESEARCH other factors affecting performance.
* Stage 5 – REVIEW findings in Stages 1 to 4.
* Stage 6 – REVISIT your investments regularly.

The *first stage* involves recognizing the opportunity. If your priority is to protect your funds against inflation and you want ready access to cash, savings accounts are the logical choice:

* The longer you are prepared to invest your funds for, the higher the interest rate tends to be.
* Still higher rates of interest may be attainable if you are prepared to indulge in high-value transactions and/or are willing to conduct receipts and withdrawals in a cost-effective manner.

Bonds can offer a reliable long-term income stream:

* If you want to keep risk low, you should confine your attention to investment-grade bonds.
* Speculative-grade bonds can offer higher rates of return, but are also more risky.

If the objective is to grow your wealth significantly in the future, shares are a popular option:

* A quick scan of P/Es and yields can provide a means of identifying companies that may be of interest.

The other opportunity commonly pursued to increase wealth significantly is property:

* When looking for properties, decide whether you are going to be a trader, a developer, or a landlord.
* Commercial property tends to be more expensive, but can provide a more reliable long-term income stream if you intend to be a landlord.

Having identified an investment opportunity, the *second stage* focuses attention on the potential reward. If you are considering savings accounts, bear in mind that the objective is to beat inflation:

* Check the real rate of return on offer (after allowing for both tax and inflation).

Bonds can offer higher rates of return than savings accounts:

* Check the redemption yield.
* Bear in mind that you may not achieve the redemption yield if you sell the bond prior to the end of its term.

If you are investing in shares, rate of return is an unknown because nobody knows for sure how companies will perform in the future:

* Return on equity tells you how effectively the company has managed shareholders' funds in the past.
* Constructing a return on equity flowchart can provide valuable insight into a company's strengths and weaknesses.
* Interest cover and dividend cover provide insight into a company's ability to meet interest payments and maintain dividends.
* The market to book ratio provides an indication of how investors perceive the company's future trading prospects.
* Combining return on equity and the market to book ratio in a value matrix enables any company to be placed in one of four quadrants, ranging from "shining star" to "space dust."
* Comparing your forecasted market to book ratio against the current market to book ratio provides a means of assessing the share price.

In the case of property, planning is key:

* Estimate the revenue and cost streams.
* If you're a property developer, allow for contingency and beware of budget creep.
* Calculate the rate of return.
* Rework the anticipated rate of return to see whether it can be improved by using debt.

Risk is the issue to be addressed in the *third stage*. Although many people regard savings accounts as being almost risk free, reality says that they are not:

✳ Select your financial institutions carefully.
✳ Consider spreading your savings over several institutions.

If you are attracted by the higher rates of return offered by bonds, there are two particularly significant risks:

✳ If you anticipate having to sell bonds prior to their redemption date, don't forget that bond prices move in the opposite direction to interest rate changes.
✳ The issuer could default, so always check their credit rating (if available).

When it comes to shares, there are three strategies that can significantly reduce risk:

✳ Focus on long-term gains rather than short-term price movements.
✳ Spread your investments over several companies (ideally in different industries).
✳ Make sure that you understand a little about the business itself (including keeping abreast of business news).

Particular attention has to be paid to risk if you're investing in property, as you're investing a large amount of money in a single asset. The key to reducing risk here is careful planning:

*   If you're adopting a buy to sell strategy, check the profit margin to ensure that it is adequate to cover any adverse price movements.
*   If you're adopting a buy to rent strategy, sensitivity analysis provides a simple but effective method for assessing the robustness of your rental income and cost estimates.

It is the first three stages of the 6R approach that tend to take up the most time, but although they're not as time consuming, the last three stages are just as important. The *fourth stage* involves researching the other factors that affect investment performance: liquidity, term, and capital.

If you're putting money into a savings account, the interest rates offered can vary according to the liquidity, term, and minimum capital requirements:

*   Check the terms and conditions.

If you're looking at bonds, it is essential that they match your cash needs in terms of timing and capital investment:

*   Confirm the redemption date and the minimum investment.
*   Consider constructing a bond ladder if you intend to generate a long-term income stream.

Shares are reasonably liquid (although you might incur a loss if you decide to sell them at short notice):

*   Set out your objectives at the outset in terms of what you want to achieve and over what period, so that you always have an exit strategy.

If you're considering property, bear in mind that it is the most illiquid of all the wealth-creating assets:

* Remember that you will be committing a significant sum into a single asset potentially for several months (if you're a trader or developer) or years (if you're a landlord).

The *fifth stage* is where your judgment comes into play. You must look at what you have learned about the investment opportunity in terms of general features, potential rewards, the associated risks, and the other factors that have an impact on performance. It is up to you to decide whether or not the investment opportunity meets your needs. If you've been diligent in addressing the preceding four stages, making the decision should not be too difficult.

Even when you've made your decision and parted with your money, the process is not over; circumstances can and indeed do change. The *sixth stage* requires you to revisit your investments regularly. Personally, I find that once a month is adequate: this keeps the time commitment low, but can also be a heartening exercise when investments are seen to be delivering returns. It would be such a shame to do all the hard work required in the first five stages and then let complacency undo all your efforts.

So there you have it. These are the principles, the opportunities, and the techniques that will help you become a successful independent investor and grow your own money. This is where the book finishes and you take over. Just remember this – you can't win if you don't play!

THE ESSENTIALS

* **Construct a personal balance sheet – identify how much you're worth right now and then prepare a balance sheet annually to monitor your progress.**
* **Choose the wealth-creating assets that are right for you – review the returns and tradeoffs available on each of the big four investment opportunities.**
* **Apply the 6R approach – be disciplined when assessing and managing investment opportunities.**

INDEX

ABOUT THE AUTHOR

David Meckin is Managing Director of Insight Financial Consulting. Previously he held several senior management positions up to and including that of finance director of a multinational business, working with companies in the UK, Europe, North America, and Asia.

He holds a degree in economics, and is a Member of the Chartered Management Institute, a Fellow of the Association of Chartered Certified Accountants, and a Fellow of the Chartered Institute of Bankers. As Managing Director of Insight Financial Consulting he regularly delivers management workshops and presents at conferences, both in the UK and abroad. He also coaches CEOs and senior executives in a variety of organizations.

Over the years he has developed a reputation for turning complexity into simplicity, making the world of finance and investment interesting, easy to understand, and even fun!

David is the author of *Naked Finance* (also from Nicholas Brealey Publishing), which provides non-financial managers with the skill sets and understanding they need to make financially sound managerial decisions. The book has been published in a number of languages including Japanese, Chinese, Russian, Korean, Indonesian, Czech, and Dutch.

In addition to regular mountaineering trips, David enjoys a variety of activities including flying (he is a qualified pilot), adventure travel, and photography.